Discover Your
ANCESTORS

DEBRETT
Founded 1769

... die octobris baptiz Elex filia Willimus Dunt

... die Novembris baptiz Willimus filius Thome ...

8 die Martij baptiz Rithardus filius Johis Bott...

7 die Aprilis baptiz Willimus filius Willmu G...

...mo die Marij baptiz Doritie filia Jenifer ...

2 die Maij baptiz Willmus filius Gwalter ...

... die Junij baptiz Maria filia Willm bond ...

... die mensis eiusd baptiz Thome filius Roberto...

... die Julij baptiz Isabll filia Thome Dompto...

... die August baptiz Johains filius Rito Whittl...

3 die August baptiz Johains filius Henrij Hylor...

6 die octobris baptiz Anna filia Thome Wapen...

...mo die Novembris baptiz Jana filia Johnis fai...

9 die Januarij baptiz Elizabete filia Thome G...

... die Julij baptiz Rithardus filius Rito Pitt...

... die Septembris baptiz Rogero filius Willa...

7 die eiusd baptiz Willmus filius Johanis ...

... die eiusd baptiz Willmus filius Wo... Bake...

9 die Novembris baptiz Johana filia Johan b...

... die Decembris baptiz Johana filia Johis Thom ...

... die Januarij baptiz Thome filius Johan Hpathe...

... die eiusd baptiz Johana filia Willmu Boo...

3 die Februarij baptiz Thome filius Thome Wat...

5 die eiusd baptiz Jente filia Rito Jutting...

Discover Your

ANCESTORS

A Quest for Your Roots

———

HUGH PESKETT

Head Genealogist of *Debrett*

ARCO PUBLISHING COMPANY, INC
219 Park Avenue South, New York, NY 10003

Published by Arco Publishing Company, Inc.
219 Park Avenue South, New York, New York 10003

LIBRARY OF CONGRESS CATALOGING IN PUBLICATION DATA

Peskett, Hugh.
Discover Your Ancestors.

Bibliography: p. 80.
1. Genealogy. 2. United States – – Genealogy – – Handbooks, manuals, etc.
I. Title.

CS16.P45   929′.1′072073   77-25264
ISBN 0-668-04529-9
ISBN 0-668-04531-0 pbk.

Printed in the United States of America

Designed by The Compton Press Ltd,
The Old Brewery, Tisbury, Wiltshire, England, for Debrett's Peerage Ltd,
23 Mossop Street, London SW3, England.

Contents

PREFACE   vii

I   GETTING STARTED   I

Why do it? – Immigration: population of the United States;
1607–1800; 1800–40; After 1840; Canada's population –
Starting with the Family.

II REGISTERS AND VITAL RECORDS   10

Primary Sources – State or Government Records: Birth;
Death; Marriage – Church and other Local Records:
Baptisms; Marriages; Burials; Gravestones and Memorials –
Finding the Records: Territories covered by Registers – Copies
and Indexes of Registers – Availability and Access.

III CENSUS AND WILLS   28

Census Records: United States Federal Census Records;
Canada; British Isles; Continental Europe; Format – Wills
and Probate Records: Probate Courts; Format.

IV LAND DEEDS   40

Government Grants – Private Transactions – National
Variations – Court Rolls and Leases.

V   OTHER USEFUL RECORDS   49

Military Records: Colonial Period; Revolutionary War;
British Army and Navy – Marriage Licenses – Other Church
Records.

VI   IMMIGRATION RECORDS AND RESEARCH   57

*Immigrants arriving after about 1820: Census; Homestead
Act; Ships' Passenger Lists; Emigration Passenger Lists;
Naturalization; Political Geography of Europe – Earlier
Immigration: Quakers; Scotch-Irish; Early Puritans of
New England.*

VII   PUTTING IT ALL TOGETHER   69

*Types of Pedigree – Source References and Research Methods
– Finding more about where they lived.*

Appendix A   HERALDRY AND COATS OF ARMS   77

Appendix B   REFERENCE SOURCES   80

Preface

THERE HAVE been a number of books written on the subject of genealogy and tracing ancestry recently. This sets out to be different from most of them. Other books on the subject tend to be either by amateurs or by academics. Running a busy professional office – with clients from all over the world, wanting research carried out all over the world – I see it from, possibly, a rather different viewpoint.

A good number of our clients, like those of most professional genealogists, in the *Debrett* offices in both Europe and America are amateurs who have "got stuck". It is with thought about the points on which amateurs tend to go astray in their researches, that I have placed some of the emphasis in this book. I have tried to give an approach for genealogists, both amateur and professional which is perhaps at least new; I hope it is also better.

In APPENDIX B, I have set out a reference guide for Europe and North America which aims not so much to give readers the information, but to tell them where they could find it. For example, the Norwegian government gives enquirers a very detailed leaflet about genealogy in Norway. My approach in this book has been to tell readers where to obtain such a leaflet, rather than to give them the information in it.

My grateful thanks are due to a number of people. To my great-great-grandfather, whose family bible first triggered off my interest; to my wife, who had to live with me while I was writing it; to Mr Milton Gladstone of Arco, whose enthusiasm was the driving force behind this book; to Mr H. B. Brooks-Baker and Mr Robert Jarman of Debrett's Peerage Ltd for their support; to my two personal assistants and my secretary, Christopher Ward, Robert Barrett and Constance Mitchell-Hedges, without whom I could have done nothing; and last, but not least, to Julian Berry and his staff at The Compton Press, who took on the real problems.

HUGH PESKETT

Parchment Street, Winchester, England
October 1977

I

Getting Started

Why do it?

AN INTEREST in ancestry is nothing new; it is really one of the oldest of human traditions and we come across it in the earliest of our records. The first book of the Bible recites the genealogy of the patriarchs, and the first chapter of the Gospel of St Matthew recites the genealogy of Jesus. Even the *Anglo-Saxon Chronicle* begins with the descents of the pagan Saxon chieftains, and all over the world, primitive races which had not learnt to read and write were able, none the less, to tell of their ancestors simply from memory. But modern men and women have an extra need; we want to know where we belong, where we come from. Two hundred years ago people did not move about so much as they do today; most people knew where they belonged without needing to think about it, because grandfather probably lived just over the next hill, and he remembered his grandfather living in the same place. Many people now, however, move every few years or so, and we often do not have anywhere of our own of which we can really say "this is where we belong, and where we come from", unless we really set to and find out.

It is a wonderful experience to know this; to go to some distant church – perhaps a continent away from where you live – look at the font and be able to say "that is where my ancestors were baptized; they stood before those altar rails to be married and they lie buried under the tombstones outside in the churchyard"; to visit the district archives and perhaps read the will they made and signed, the deeds of the land they farmed and the lists of the taxes they paid. Our ancestors were not just names on a pedigree chart, but were real *people*, with all of the problems and worries we have today – and probably a great deal more besides. What were the problems they left behind, what were the hopes they had for the future, which led them to leave home and set out for a new life in another continent? Sometimes the answers can emerge from your researches.

There is something too of the thrill of all detection, the piecing together of clues until you solve the mystery of that missing ancestor. In the case of the early New Englander whose English origins had been hunted by genealogists for 80 years, the answer emerged that his father had disagreed with his widowed grandmother about the family farm, and had left home for a few years – during this time the child was born for which everyone had been hunting. This detective work, though, is unlike any other because you are personally involved.

America and Canada are new countries; apart from the Red Indians and the Esquimaux everyone traces from immigrants from somewhere else in the world. Sooner or later every American or Canadian ancestry research project is going to end up at the harbourside or the beach. Then the research is going to have to take the great leap over the ocean; usually over the Atlantic to Europe or Africa, but some immigrants came from Asia or Australia and New Zealand, over the Pacific. This is what makes American and Canadian genealogy so interesting, as you never know what you are going to uncover or where your researches are going to take you. America has been called "the Great Melting Pot" and immigration is such an important part of American genealogy that we must start by seeing just what it amounts to.

Immigration

THE POPULATION OF THE UNITED STATES is over 200 million, and they trace back to about 39 million immigrants who are their ancestors. Most of this increase has been since 1800 and so has most of the immigration.

On the other hand, the earlier settlers have more descendants because they have been here longer and for more generations. Exact figures are hard to come by because there are no detailed immigration records of early settlers and some suspicion that the later ones are not as complete as they should be. We can, however, summarize the figures:

1607–1800. In 1800 the population of the United States was about four million. These were the descendants of about 750,000 immigrants since the first Jamestown settlement in 1607. The earliest settlers were almost entirely English (or Welsh), followed by about 200,000 "Scotch-Irish" (Presbyterian settlers from the north of Ireland, whose ancestors had settled there from Scotland 100 years earlier). The Scotch-Irish did not start coming over until about 1717, 100 years and more after the first English arrived. They were followed by about 200,000 from Germany, principally the so-called "Palatines" from the Rhineland area of Germany; and there were some smaller groups from other countries, such as the French, mainly Protestant, Huguenots in South Carolina and Catholics in Louisiana. As well as these there were about 750,000 black people of African origin, mostly slaves.

1800–40. Another million immigrants arrived, three-quarters of them from the British Isles, and the other quarter from Germany.

AFTER **1840**. It was only after 1840 that immigration into the United States turned from a trickle into a flood; 95% of all immigration into America has been since 1840. Many ethnic groups who are important today have only been represented in America since then. The British continued to come, four million of them came in this period; four-and-a-half-million Irish; one-and-a-half-million Germans; and a million French, to add to those who had come before. They were joined by two-and-a-half-million Scandinavians, mostly to the Mid-West. It was after about 1880 – especially up to 1914 – that there came what was the greatest migration in the history of the human race. Since 1800, about 28 million people have come to America, amounting to about 70% of all immigrants who have come here. Five-and-a-half-million Italians, four million Poles and other Slav races – we do not have exact figures as the statistics were based on the governments as they were then. Poland, for example, did not have a separate existence, being ruled partly by Russia, partly by the Austro-Hungarian Empire, and partly by what was Prussia and later Germany. Therefore there are no separate figures for Polish immigration: Poles may be listed as Russians, Austrians or Germans. To some extent this applies to others; for instance, an estimated two million Jews and one-and-a-half-million Russians. Four million Canadians have immigrated to the United States, and they themselves were of previous immigrant origin.

In terms of the modern population of the United States the earlier settlers have more descendants than the later ones : British settlers have contributed 50% and German settlers 10% of the ancestry of modern Americans; while 82% have at least one British and 17% at least one German ancestral line in their pedigrees. The other 40% of American ancestry is contributed by the several other ethnic origins.

CANADA'S POPULATION is over 22 million; about one-third of them are of British origin, one-third French, and the other third various other nationalities, of which – much like the United States – Germans are the most numerous. Canadian genealogy is more important to Americans than these statistics suggest, because so many present-day Americans have got Canadian ancestors. The earlier Canadian immigrants were almost entirely French or British. A very high proportion of the British ones were from Scotland; many of these went to Nova Scotia, which had been a French province called Acadia. The French inhabitants were expelled, going to Louisiana, where they were called "Cajuns" (*i.e.* Acadians). There was also migration the other way, of Empire Loyalists who fled to Canada from the United States after the Revolution, and just to complicate things further, some of their descendants have migrated back again to the United States.

What this pattern of migration means is that a great many Americans and Canadians are only second or third-generation descendants of the original immigrants, probably as many as two-thirds of the population. So far as tracing their immigrant ancestors' origins is concerned, they are the lucky ones because there are usually enough traditional memories in the family to take their research back to Europe or wherever they came from without the need of much research in America. For those whose family traditions are not enough, there are ample census, immigration, naturalization and shipping records to fill the gaps; their research can make a fine beginning. It is a sound principle in genealogy that the earlier the research goes in time, the harder it becomes. It is for the 20% or so of Americans whose ancestors were here in the Colonial period, before the Revolution, that the American research is difficult.

Starting with the Family

All genealogy is fundamentally a matter of starting the research from a basis of known facts and working backwards in time from that basis to establish more and earlier facts. This is why it is so important to make a start in the right way. You will always want to start – unless someone has done some research on your family before – by asking the family all that they know, collecting up together everything they remember or what they *think* they remember. (You cannot always rely on this material because old people put out of their minds the things they would rather forget, and tend to glorify and exaggerate other things.) Sometimes you will find family bibles and other records; these tend to be more reliable than memory, but they can have pitfalls. My own family bible includes entries back to 1798, though it is actually the bible given to my great-grandparents as a wedding present in 1871. What they did was to copy out entries back to 1798 from another, older, bible. Some of the entries in the family bible did not agree with the official and church records, so I made some enquiries and I tracked down the older bible in my grandmother's attic containing the original entries. What had happened was that, in 1871, my great-grandmother had made one or two mistakes in copying out the older entries. The lesson is to check everything if you can – though often this is not possible – and bear in mind that many items are not 100% accurate. Also some families are simply not interested; I have just mentioned my father's family who kept a family bible going back to 1798, but my mother's family were so uninterested that my mother had never even been told where her own father was born.

Perhaps even more in need of checking is where someone in the family did a considerable amount of research a long time ago. This is especially tricky as in those days – the 1890s always impress me as a bad period for it – people were less critical and more inclined to accept the answer which suited them, rather than the answer which actually fitted the facts. You would be amazed at how many Adams families researched in the 1890s conveniently joined up to the Presidential Adamses; even if it meant stretching some facts beyond what was biologically possible, such as assuming a man was a grandfather before he was 20 years old. It is no use compiling a family history based simply on wishful thinking and what you want it to be; it has to correspond to the facts, and nothing else will do. In the past, perhaps people were not so critical about facts in genealogy, so it is certainly a wise step to check anything about which you are in the least doubtful. It is particulary vital because these facts you are assembling represent the foundation of your own research, and wrong "starting information" for your researches can mean that everything you do will be wasted. Not long ago a client of ours came to the office to engage us for professional research and gave me the details, which he assured me were correct, about his grandfather. After he had spent a fair amount of money and we had produced a long pedigree for the man he had asked us to research, he told us that he now realized he had given us the wrong name for his own grandfather. All the research we had done and all the money he had paid us were wasted, as we had been given wrong starting information by the client and had traced the ancestry of the wrong man.

Easy assumptions are just as misleading. People always tend to assume things in the past were similar to the way they are today. A typical example is age at marriage. Before about 1800, people generally married much later than they do now; the average age of marriage was, for most of the period which covers the body of genealogical work, between 28 and 30. I well remember one case on which I worked, dealing with an early Puritan immigrant to Massachusetts. Our client provided a date of birth for the settler which he assured us was correct, but gave us no reason for the date, apart from quoting a researcher who had worked on the case some years before. In the end, I discovered that this date of birth on which I was supposed to base my research had been calculated on nothing more than that the date of marriage of the settler was known. Everyone had assumed, without evidence, that the man had married at about the age of 22 or 23. Actually, as we were to discover, he had married quite late, when aged 44. Everyone had been researching at periods 20 years or so later than they should have done, simply because of an assumption which was really no better than a wild guess.

Another example was where we knew of a William B. who had married when he was aged 25. 27 years later we knew of the marriage of a William B. in the same place, who had five children by this marriage. Our client assumed that the second William B. was son of the marriage 27 years earlier and asked us to discover evidence of this. It turned out, however, that these Williams were not father and son, but one man. He married twice, once when aged 25; his wife was childless, and after she died, when he was aged 52, he married again, to a much younger bride, and in his fifties became the father of five children.

The lesson of this is that you must never assume anything in genealogy; it is essential to remember that the people we research were not just names on pieces of paper or parchment, with set patterns and performances, but had all the fascinating individual characteristics of real living people. Above all, they did not always behave as we would expect or think they ought to have done. Anyway, if they had, research would be much less enjoyable; the unpredictability keeps a researcher alert.

What you have to do, therefore, is to collect up all of your "starting information", which will be mostly either what the family remembers or, if you are lucky, some previous research results as well. Then get it all sorted out and properly listed (*see* CHAPTER VII, "Putting it All Together"). Most families know their genealogy back to their grandparents. This is about as far as many of us remember; but sometimes elderly relations can remember a little more. In 1972, I met an old lady of 95, whose grandfather had been a British officer in the War of 1812. I heard from her the stories her grandfather had told her of the burning of Washington 160 years earlier. So sort out what you know already, or what you can find out from the family; if you are fortunate and one of the majority of Americans whose immigrant ancestors arrived in the last 100 years or so, family memories will probably take you back to research in Europe without any need to look at American records. Whichever way it is, you are now ready to start research in earnest.

II

Registers and Vital Records

THE BASIC framework of genealogy is that people were born, they grew up, married, had children and died. (Naturally, once we have established that basic framework, we can fill in the details of where they lived, what they did and how they earned their livings, but the basic framework has to come first.) In effect, the essence of research is that we start from the known, and work backwards in time into the unknown. We start with the child, identify the parents and their marriage, then to the parents in childhood, from whom we identify the grandparents and their marriage, and so on back through the earlier generations.

Primary Sources

Usually we get these pieces of information from the basic "primary sources". When a child was born its birth was *usually* recorded; it might be a government record of a birth, or a church record of baptism, a Jewish registration of circumcision, or some other source according to the country and the religion. The precise type of record, however, is not so important; what matters is that we have a record of date, place, and parents for each birth – allowing for the fact that baptisms are dated later than births. In much the same way, we can get a record of the marriage of the parents named in the record of the child's birth – naturally remembering that not all parents were married. This has the advantage for research that at least more modern records of marriage name the father – if not the mother as well – of all the brides and bridegrooms, which obviously gives us a good start on to the next generation back. The exact form of the record varies considerably between different countries and states; at different periods of time in those countries and states; and – where church records are involved – between different churches at any one time. None the less we have the three essential records of birth (or baptism), marriage, and death (or burial). We then need to know what they are and where to find them.

State or Government Records

These are called different names in different places and countries. Americans call them "Vital Records" or "Vital Statistics". In Britain, people refer to "Civil Registration" or the "General Register Office", or talk of local "Registrars"; and, of course, in other countries speaking other languages they have various names. In the modern period, these are virtually the only records a genealogist will use, as almost everywhere in the world today governments undertake this official record-keeping. What is meant by "modern" varies: in France, the government began this in 1792; in England and Wales in 1837; while in the United States, Massachusetts began a centralized system in 1844 but Georgia did not until 1919. It should be remembered, though, that many New England towns, and several American cities kept local records much earlier than state-wide records were kept. Boston town meeting registers, for example, started in 1639, and New Orleans city in 1790. The form of record also varies.

BIRTH registrations include almost invariably the place and date of birth, the name of the child, the names of the parents and the mother's maiden name. Beyond that there is substantial variation. United States standard forms omit the father's occupation, but include a great deal of medical information about the birth. Australian ones – and the most recent type in use in England – include the birthplaces of both parents as well, for which genealogists will always be thankful.

DEATH registrations also vary between the minimum given in the older English format, which states only the date and place of death, the name and age of the deceased with the cause of death – plus the technical details of the registration – to some Australian registrations which go into full details of the parentage, birthplace, marriage and children of the deceased.

MARRIAGE is the most variable record of all. Even now, some States do not have state-wide registration of marriages. Many others record only the minimum of details, the date, place, and the name of the parties and no more. On the other hand, many Scottish marriage registrations include such details as the age, birthplace and parentage of the bride and 'groom.

Church and other Local Records

BEFORE governments became involved in vital records and registration, most records were kept by churches – although there tended to be government interference in church record-keeping. In both England and France there was control by Acts and Royal Decrees, and in Sweden, the government, rather than setting up civil registrars, delegated the task to the established church with official status (there was a similar situation in Quebec up to 1926). The idea of an "Established

Baptismal entries (in Latin) in Selborne parish register 1585-88
(Courtesy, Vicar of Selborne)

Anno dñi 1585

4ᵗ die Julij baptiz Johana filia Johanis Bridges —
18 die Julij baptiz Johana filius Johñs Nicholñ —
25 die Julij baptiz Elizabethe filia Thome Oxford
26 die September baptiz Annis filia Henrij Nicholñ
10 die octobris baptiz Elior filia Willmus Spente —
21 die Novembris baptiz Willmus filius Thome Grano

Anno 1586
18 die martij baptiz Richardus filius Johñis Bottoll
19 die Aprilis baptiz Willmus filius Willmi Goāne
primo die maij baptiz Davidis filia Jenfer woolege
22 die maij baptiz Willmus filius Gwalter thamberly
8 die Junij baptiz Maria filia Willm bone
10 die menssis eiusdē baptiz Thome filius Robarte prewin
3ᵉ die Julij baptiz Isable filia Thome Dompton
9ᵉ die August baptiz Johañs filius Rito Whppe
13 die August baptiz Johañs filius Henrij Holoway
26 die octobris baptiz Anna filia Thome Vapenter filiu
primo die novembris baptiz Hana filia Johñs faith ful

Anno 1587
29 die Januarij baptiz Elizabeth filia Thome Stoffid
3ᵉ die Julij baptiz Richardus filius Rito Pittett
10 die Septembris baptiz Rogro filius Wm Taylor
17 die eiusdē baptiz Willmus filius Johañs Fidor
20 die eiusdē baptiz Willmus filius Wm Bikeer
19 die Novembris baptiz Johana filia Johañs bridger
6 die Decembris baptiz Johana filia Johñ Thore —
4ᵉ die Januarij baptiz Thome filius Johañ Hartror
21 die eiusdē baptiz Johanla filia Willmn Boon

Anno 1588
23 die ffebruarij baptiz Thome filius Thome Vapenter
25 die eiusdē baptiz ffranta filia Rito Passinger
4ᵉ die martij baptiz Johanla filia Mathew Dante —
9ᵉ die eiusdē baptiz Hana filia Willmus Dante —
12 die eiusdē baptiz Thome filius Thome Nicholñ
4ᵉ die Aprilis baptiz Rogro filius Rogro Taylor
2ᵈ die August menssis baptiz Als filia Johan Hartyn Hartoll

Church" is strange to many Americans – although it would not have been 200 years ago. In most European countries one Church had an official status and government backing: in England, it was the (Protestant Episcopalian) "Church of England"; in Scotland, the (Presbyterian) "Church of Scotland"; in Scandinavian countries it was the Lutheran Church; while in most of Southern Europe it was the Roman Catholic Church, and in Eastern Europe, the Eastern Orthodox Church. In America, this principle was imported in the colonial period, when in Virginia and the South, the Protestant Episcopalian Church was so closely linked to the government as to be effectively "Established"; and in New England, the Independent or Congregational Church had a similar status. Not uncommonly in Europe, legal measures enforced the status of the Established Church, sometimes quite harshly; huge fines were imposed for failure to marry or have children baptized by Church of England ceremonies; and Catholic France persecuted the Protestant Huguenots, for example. Such intolerance could also be found in America – some early Quakers were hanged for their beliefs in New England.

This means that from a research point of view, there was a more or less unified set of records for each district in such countries – even before the beginning of state keeping of vital records or registration. The United States Constitution, however, proclaimed liberty of religion, and, though the situation did not change at once in some parts of New England, there had been, even before the Declaration of Independence, a growing number of other Churches. These included the Quakers in Pennsylvania, Lutherans from Germany in Pennsylvania and in South Carolina, and Presbyterian "Scotch-Irish" immigrants in Pennsylvania and Virginia. French Canada and Louisiana were naturally Catholic, and there were small groups of Jews, Moravians, Huguenots and others.

With all these numerous Churches it follows that there were consequently several separate series of registers being kept in any one place. It is quite possible that your ancestors might have changed Church more than once – especially on the Frontier, where the question was far more often what Church was available, rather than which one you chose. In any event, if you do not know to which Church they belonged, it may well involve searching several registers. It is helpful to know the affiliations of some different denominations; in general, Catholics kept apart from Protestants, and Jews kept themselves entirely separate. Methodists began as a revival movement within the Episcopalian Church, so many Methodists began life as Episcopalians; on the other hand, John Wesley, founder of the Methodists, had close links with Moravians in Georgia, and many Quakers, if they ceased that membership, became Methodists. Presbyterians, Congregationalists and Baptists had much in common in earlier years – indeed in England they did form a single "United Dissenters" body for a time. Most immigrants kept to the Church of their homeland, especially in their earlier years in America, and so, for example, most Scandinavians were Lutherans to begin with, even if they changed later; the same is true for other nationalities. The entries in the registers also vary.

BAPTISMS were the normal church record of the arrival of new children in a family. It should be remembered that this was primarily a record of church membership and not a record made for genealogists. Most children were baptized within a few weeks of birth; a weak baby thought to be in danger of dying might be baptized, in accordance with some doctrines, immediately it was born. Thus, apart from the question of exact date of birth – which is not, after all, an essential item of information for a genealogist – a baptism is just as good as a

Births Anno 1654

Elizabeth Petty the Daughter of John Petty of Pucknall by Eliz: his wife was borne the last day of January:

Elizabeth Bayley the daughter of Willm Bayley by Joane his wife was borne the ffifth day of ffebruary

Margarett Rieues the Daughter of Robert Rieues of Hursley by Susan his wife was borne the Twelueth day of ffebruary

Mary the daughter of Gyles Frodd of Marden by Joane his wife was borne the Nineteenth day of ffebruary:

Margarett the Daughter of John King of Crampmere by Margarett his wife was borne the Twentieth day of ffebruary:

Daniell the Sonne of John Browne of Baddesley by Christian his wife was borne the ffourth day of March:

Elizabeth Simes the Daughter of Thomas Simes of Standen by Elizabeth his wife was borne ye Tenth day of March:

Anno 1655

Alice Locke the Daughter of James Locke of Hursley streete by Anne his wife was borne the Tenth day of Aprill:

Richard the Sonne of Robert Crouth of Standen by Sara his wife, was borne the ffoure & Twentieth of Aprill

Alice the Daughter of William Morrant of Cadwell by Eliz: his wife was borne ye same 24th day of Aprill:

registration of birth. For doctrinal reasons, however, some records vary from this norm. Baptists are opposed to the baptism
of infants, believing that this should take place later in life, when
the candidate is old enough to be aware of his or her own
beliefs. Their records of baptism are therefore of limited
genealogical value, but many Baptist congregations kept birth
registers as well. The Society of Friends (Quakers) do not
believe in baptism at all, though they keep outstandingly good
records of births. Jews do not have a relevant baptism ceremony, but many synagogues kept registers of births, although
some have registers only of circumcision (at eight days old) of
infant boys. Jewish marriage records, however, commonly give
so much detail of the parentage of the bride and 'groom that
the defects of birth records can be overcome. Baptism (or similar) register entries vary; at one extreme you may find, un-
helpfully, simply the date and "John Smith was baptized";
more usually, you will find "John the son of William Smith",
or "John the son of William and Mary Smith", or, even
better, "John the son of William and Mary Smith of Green
Valley". How much detail you get is as much a matter of luck
as anything else. Scottish Presbyterians and German Lutherans normally add the valuable information of the mother's
maiden name, and some of the American Lutheran registers
even add details of the immigrant family's origins in Germany.

MARRIAGES are, generally speaking, less well recorded in America than they are in Europe. Many American Churches seem
to have kept very little in the way of early marriage registers,
and a genealogist has to fall back on marriage licenses and
bonds in county court-houses. There are far fewer doctrinal

---

*Birth entries (in English) in Hursley parish register under the Common-
wealth 1654-55* (Courtesy, Vicar of Hursley)

Banns of Marriage between _Richard Bavidge_ of the _Parish of Ruishell_ in this County

and _Elizabeth Bond_ of this Parish were published in this Church _Sep: 18. 25. Oct: 2 1774_

No   _Richard Bavidge_ ——————— of the Parish _of Ruishell in the County of_
        Southampton ———————— and _Elizabeth Bond_ ——————— of said
Parish ——————————————————————————————————————— were

Married in this _Church_ ——— by _Banns_ ——————————————————
this _twenty first_ ——— Day of _October_ ——————— in the Year One Thouſand Seven
Hundred and _seventy four_ ——— by me _C. Corlett, Curate_

This Marriage was ſolemnized between Us $\left\{\begin{array}{l}\text{The mark of Richard Bavidge} \\ \text{the mark} \Rightarrow \text{of Elizabeth Bond}\end{array}\right.$

In the Preſence of _Richd Hurst_
                        Benjn Earle

differences over marriage than there are over baptism and so much less variation in the details recorded. Some of the earliest English marriage registers may be so "male chauvinist" as to omit the bride's name entirely, simply recording "William Smith and his wife were married"; but usually the register records "William Smith and Mary Brown were married". Some records include parents of the bride and groom, for instance Quakers and many Scottish registers. By and large, the amount of additional detail is again largely a question of luck, depending upon the time and trouble the clerk was willing to take. Sometimes government attempts at control appear. In England, for example, elopements and secret marriages were becoming rather out of hand and an Act to control them meant that between 1754 and 1837, every marriage, to be lawful, had to be celebrated by the Established Church of England ceremony – making exceptions only for Quakers and Jews – and recorded on special forms printed by the government printer, which the bride and groom and their witnesses had to sign.

BURIALS are particularly poorly recorded in America (and, for that matter, in Scotland). One reason for this was that so many burials in America were not in centralized public graveyards and churchyards – as is usual in Europe – but were private burial places, where probably only the family at the nearby house were buried. Church registers of burials are, in general, only of limited value to a genealogist as so often they record only a date and the name. One important value of burial records, however, is to eliminate the possibility of error in identifying as your ancestor a child which had died young – a

Marriage entry in Itchen Abbas parish register
(Courtesy, Rector of Itchen Abbas)

significant possibility when so many children died in infancy or childhood. When a burial register records ages at death, though, it is of special value, as from age at death a researcher can calculate the approximate date of birth of the person in question, which narrows down the search for a baptism or birth record. The extent to which this is recorded varies; it became compulsory, for example, in England following an Act in 1812.

GRAVESTONES AND MEMORIALS can often be a valuable supplement to burial records, because many of them record far more detail than the registers; often ages, dates of birth, and even relationships and birthplaces are given. Jewish gravestones have the special complication of the Hebrew language and script, as well as the Jewish calendar. Quakers often had a testimony against memorials – and some of their early memorials, before that testimony was developed, were buried in Quaker graveyards.

Finding the Records

It can often be a research project of its own to find where the records you need actually are, before you can start the actual genealogy by using the records. The whereabouts vary from state or country to country, county to county, and even in one town between different churches. It is crucial, as without knowing where to find the records you cannot do your research; some successful researchers have achieved their results as much by knowing where to find the records as by using them. Naturally government administered state-wide vital records and registration are the best organized. In the United States and Canada, these are usually in the state or provincial capitals; for many European countries they are in the capital cities such as London, England and Edinburgh, Scotland. In many continental European countries the records are in regional or provincial centres, as in France, Germany, Italy and the Scandinavian countries. When it comes to local and church registers, however, the situation is much less systematic.

In European countries with an Established Church, government authority has meant that a good deal of their care and custody is well controlled. In Scotland, for instance, all the older registers of the Presbyterian Church of Scotland are deposited centrally in Edinburgh, but much less provision is made for the other, non-established Churches. In England most (but not all) of the earlier registers of the "nonconformist" (*i.e.* non-established) Churches are in the government archives in London, and the (Protestant Episcopalian) Church of England registers are in process of being collected into the county record offices. The registers of the Scandinavian Churches are also being collected into regional archives. Where the Roman Catholic Church is involved, there is generally much less collection of registers into archives and in the predominantly Catholic countries most of the registers are still held by the local parish priests.

In the United States there is much less gathering of registers into archives – though some momentum towards this is developing – and this means that most of the registers are still in the local churches. Alternatively they may even be in private hands, as there has not been the legislation that there has been in many European countries to protect registers. Sometimes the church itself no longer exists. In most of Canada the circumstances are the same, with church registers being kept locally without any real system or organization, but in Quebec things are different. This is because both the predominant Catholic and minority Protestant priests and ministers up to 1926 had official status as keepers of vital records, so they had the government authority and control which you find in some

Established Churches in European countries. Indeed it is the French background to Quebec which makes its records so different.

New England town meeting registers are in many ways unique, as they fulfil the function which state vital records had later, and which church registers had especially in Europe. The system, in fact, had much in common with the contemporary Puritan government in England under which, for about six years, virtually identical civil registers were kept in the 1650s. These will be found in the town hall at the place in question.

Some countries had a system of duplicating records, and this, where it happened, makes for, first, greater certainty of the record having survived – which is always one of the problems – and, secondly, the duplicate was usually kept in a centralized official place. In England, for example, all ministers of the Established Church of England were supposed to send in annual copies of all register entries, over the previous year, to the bishop. These are usually called "Bishop's Transcripts" and are to be found in the archives of the bishopric or diocese; most diocesan archives are in English county record offices. Beware, though, that as diocesan boundaries were not always the same as county ones, they may not be in the obvious county record office but the neighbouring one. These transcripts ought to start in 1597, but many of the early ones are lost or incomplete. Similarly in France, a Royal Decree ordered duplicate registers to be kept in 1667 and there is a similar pattern in other countries, e.g. Denmark, where duplicates were kept from 1814. There was very little of this in North America; Quebec was the notable exception, where in any case the parish registers had official status and the government required duplicates to be deposited at the district court office. There are a few fragments, too, amongst the Bishop of London's archives, in England, of Bishop's Transcripts from some Episcopalian churches in the southern states in the colonial period — unfortunately these are too fragmentary to be of much use. TERRITORIES COVERED BY REGISTERS vary greatly; in most places where there was an Established Church, there were defined areas around each church, parishes – hence "parish registers" – and the New England town meeting registers were similarly related to the boundaries of the township. One must stress again that genealogy is concerned with people, to whom the theoretical restrictions of parish boundaries were no definition of which church they attended. Perhaps there was another church easier to get to or the church they always went to when they were children was not far away. Perhaps they did not like the minister or the length of his sermons conflicted with the hardness of the seats. In any event, never expect the people you are looking for to be rigidly and precisely in the registers of the church the map says they ought to have used. Moreover, they may have changed Church. I have known a couple, brought up as Presbyterians, who had three children, one each baptized in the Episcopalian, Methodist and Congregational churches.

When you are dealing, however, with the other churches, which were not "established" with government authority and defined territories, there is much less precision or certainty about which registers relate to which district. Some ministers – especially if they were great preachers – would travel about a great deal, and I have known such a man who kept his own personal register, recording children he had baptized as far apart as a 50 mile radius around his home. Sometimes too a minister would take his register with him when he transferred to a new place. This was specially prevalent on the Frontier.

In Ireland, always a place where things genealogical which should be, *are not*, and things which should not be, *are* – having Irish ancestry myself, I know it only too well – there is a particular complication. The (Protestant Episcopalian) Church of Ireland, to which less than 10% of the population belonged, had one series of parishes and boundaries. Being the Established Church, these parish boundaries were – with a few exceptions – the same boundaries as the civil government districts, and so correspond to the names of the parishes under which people were classified for taxes, censuses, and legal records. The great majority of the population were, however, Roman Catholic; there were entirely separate Catholic churches with their own parishes and usually quite different boundaries. Thus an Irish Catholic might well be found in one parish for church purposes – including registers – but an entirely different parish for legal and government purposes. Ireland is not the only country where this sort of headache occurs.

Copies and Indexes of Registers

A great many registers have been copied, even printed, and legions more have been microfilmed and indexed. A large number of New England town registers have been printed, and there has also been a considerable amount of copying and printing of registers in England. Elsewhere, while you will find some of this work being done, in general there is not a great deal of activity. What does deserve special mention is the Latter Day Saints (Mormon) Church programme for microfilming, and eventually indexing by computer, all of the genealogical records which they can collect. At present by far the largest part of their programme has been devoted to British records, and even with English registers their work has not yet reached the half-way point. It is, however, an enormous project and of a value which will increase as it becomes more complete, with the proviso – and this is a point which is emphasized by the LDS Genealogical Society officials themselves – that this is not a record but only an *index*. The great danger is that people will take the easy way out – which, like so many easy ways out in genealogy, is quite wrong – and simply take the computer printout index entries on their own, when the proper use is to take these as an index to the original records and no more. Like all indexes it has the limitation that it indexes only what is there – whereas a genealogist needs to know also what is *not* there. For example, the gap in the record, due to a page torn out or faded into illegibility, could well explain why the entry you are looking for is not there. It has also the limitation that original parish and other registers include clerical and other errors; many of the LDS microfilms are not of original registers but are of copies of originals, which inevitably include more errors of their own; then these are transcribed again into computer material, where, despite most efficient double-checking some errors will inevitably slip through.

None the less this project is truly one of the great genealogical enterprises, and so long as it is remembered that these indexes are indexes *to* and not a substitute *for* research in original records, it will become one of the greatest aids to genealogy.

The indexing of official government vital records and registers is variable to a degree. In England and Wales, for instance, there is a comprehensive index volume for each three-month period covering the entire territory. Scotland has similar indexes of civil registration; but many countries are not so well provided for. In some states in America, the indexing is so limited that it is virtually necessary to know all of the information you are going to find from the records before a copy can be produced.

Availability and Access

Normally all registers and vital records with an official status are publicly accessible and available at the appropriate office during normal working hours, although some of these offices may be closed to the public for an hour or so at either end of the working day. The same applies to church registers where these are deposited in county or state archives, and New England town meeting registers at town halls. Exactly what is available varies greatly: in some states you can read the actual registers yourself and make notes of the relevant entry; in others, the office staff carry out the search and give you the results usually on a certificate, for a fee. In certain places (*e.g.* Missouri and parts of Australia), there are privacy rules which restrict what you can see; and in others (*e.g.* England and Wales), you can read the indexes free of charge yourself, but can only get the information by paying £2.50 (about $4.45) for a fully detailed certificate.

When it comes to church registers which are not in archives, but still in the care of the priest or minister, things are much less straightforward. In the first place, you cannot expect to simply arrive at the home of the minister and be shown his registers immediately, because most ministers are busy men, with more important things to do than sit around at the convenience of any genealogist who happens to turn up. Nor has the minister any obligation to let you see the registers at all, unless he is a minister of one of the Established Churches in a country which has such a thing – and even then, while he has a legal obligation to allow you to see the registers, he can insist on reasonable warning in advance and an appointment. Most ministers will also want to sit with you while you make your search, or arrange for someone else to do so. Some Catholic priests may refuse to let you see the registers yourself but will make the searches for you. Do not be surprised at this, because there are too many examples of people having cut out pages from registers if they were ones with their ancestors entered on them, or even writing in forged entries to prove a pedigree they do not have. There is also the point that many priests and ministers are opposed to the doctrines of the Mormon Church and may be reluctant to allow their registers to be searched by Mormon genealogists. I have personally experienced ministers seeking assurances that I was not a Mormon before allowing me to read their registers. Anyone wishing to read Catholic registers is well advised to obtain a letter of authority from the bishop or his vicar-general before approaching parish priests.

III

Census and Wills

ALL TOO often newcomers to genealogy tend to think that vital records and registers, the subject of the last chapter, are the only records ever used. This is understandable because their content is so useful genealogically that it is difficult for the amateur to realize that there can be anything else. My experience as a professional genealogist, however, is that registers and vital records should not as a rule occupy more than half of one's research time. The limitation of, particularly, parish registers is that while they contain intensive genealogical detail, they cover only one small district, and only one religious denomination. So a family has to move only a few miles and they disappear from that series of registers and you do not know, without much hunting around, where they have gone to or came from.

The other point which many amateur genealogists forget is that we can establish sound and proven genealogy without having the exact dates and places of births, marriages, etc. What matters is *relationship*; genealogy is more about who were the father and mother, the brothers and sisters, than it is about exact dates and places. And there are numerous other sources besides vital records and registers which can tell you these things. The most important of these are census returns and wills. These can not only identify relations, parents and children, brothers and sisters, uncles and nephews, but from the other information they supply, guide you direct to the right parish register so well informed that you arrive knowing exactly who you are looking for and at what dates.

Moreover, in so far as you can ever be dogmatic about such a variable subject as genealogical research, I would say that it is generally unsound to make any searches in parish or church registers unless you have first made any possible searches in census records; and probably also made any possible searches in wills and probate records.

Census Records

Basically a census is a government-organized list of inhabitants. Exactly what information is included varies enormously. At one extreme, it may list merely heads of households by name, with summary details of the rest of the family and anyone else living there; and, at the other extreme, it may list each individual by name, age, birthplace, occupation and add even more details. It provides, however scanty or complete the information, a treasure-house for a genealogist.

THE UNITED STATES FEDERAL CENSUS RECORDS are outstanding, and have been made even more valuable by some vast indexing projects. They began in 1790, when lists were made naming individually the heads of households only, and numbers only in each household of free white males under the age of 16, over the age of 16, free white females, other free persons and slaves. Every 10 years thereafter a new census was taken; up to 1840 the only persons actually named were the heads of households, but progressively more information was given about the other inhabitants. The real breakthrough in importance of US Census records was in 1850. In this return every person is named, with their age to the year, state of birth and a great deal of other information, including occupations, and also – a valuable clue to another class of records – whether the person owned land, and what its value was. The wealth of detail increased: in 1880 we find – in addition to everyone's relationship to the head of the family – whether the father and mother of each person was of foreign birth, and also where they were born. In 1900 the record adds how many years married, how many children, and, for immigrants, the year of immigration. What makes these even more valuable is that the complete 1900 Census has been indexed by surname and state. The 1880 Census has been indexed for those families which had children under the age of 10. Both of these indexes were by the Federal authorities and use the "Soundex" system. The 1850 Census has been indexed by the LDS (Mormon) Genealogical Society, and a great many of the other census returns have been partially or completely published and/or indexed by various organizations. Several states have incomplete returns for some of the earlier censuses, and the entire 1890 Census was destroyed in a fire. There are certain traps to be avoided, especially on the Frontier as it moved westwards; this is because territories became states. Their boundaries were changed and some were subdivided, occasionally in a highly complicated pattern. For example, North and South Dakota were part of the Louisiana Purchase of 1803 but the first census which included them was 1860 – as Dakota Territory, which then included parts of Wyoming and Montana – but they did not become separate states until 1889. Maine was part of Massachusetts until 1820, and so it is included with Massachusetts in the 1790, 1800 and 1810 returns.

There are also a few special censuses, especially of territories on the Frontier, and also such things as the 1840 Census of

Map of America showing the expansion of the United States

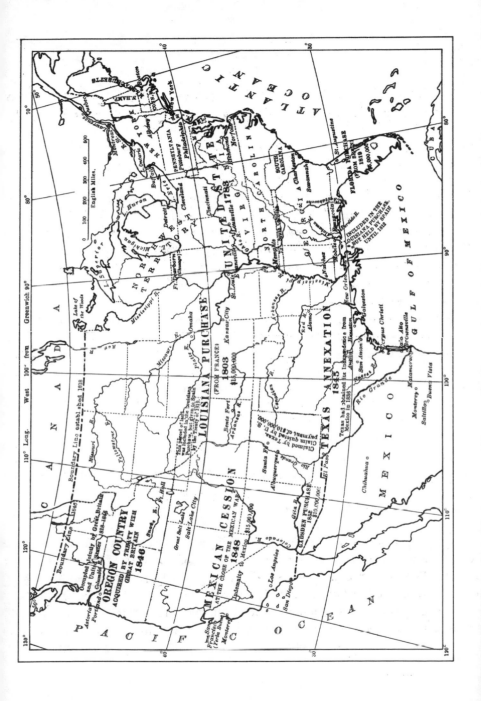

Revolutionary and Military Pensioners. Federal Census returns under 75 years old are not available for public research, but the Bureau of Census will supply limited personal information to close relations, on postal enquiry.

IN CANADA the situation is complicated because of the history, but basically there are detailed census returns for most of the eastern provinces available for one or more of 1851, 1861 and 1871; but there is nothing for the western provinces at all. Canadian censuses under 100 years old are not available, and the western provinces had inadequate population or government to achieve a census in 1871. Nova Scotia has heads of family returns from 1770 onwards, and there are also some early heads of family returns for other provinces. The former French possessions have various early returns in the period 1666 to 1739.

IN THE BRITISH ISLES the first census was made in 1801, but apart from some rare survivals, no detailed lists of persons have survived earlier than 1841. This return listed all persons by name, grouped in households, but without identifying their relationships. Ages of persons over the age of 15 were listed in five-year groupings, but exact ages were given for younger children. The record of birthplace was limited to a plain "yes" or "no" as to whether they had been born in the same county where they now lived, unless they had been born overseas. Returns every 10 years from 1851 gave much more detail; notably exact ages in years, parish and county of birth, and relationships of everyone in the house to the head of the household. In England and Wales, censuses under 100 years old (*i.e.* after 1871) are not available for public research, but there are special arrangements for searches in the returns up to 1901 by the officials on postal requests. In Scotland, the returns up to ˙ⁿ ˙ are open to the public. In Ireland, all returns earlier th.... 1901 – with a few exceptions – were lost in a fire, but the 1901 and 1911 returns are open for public research. Although politically Ireland has been divided into Northern Ireland and the Republic since 1921, all the returns for the north are still in Dublin, in the south.

CONTINENTAL EUROPEAN censuses vary considerably and one complication is recent political history. Germany, for example, became a united country only in 1871, and many of the records of a number of European countries which came into existence only after the break-up of the Russian, Turkish, and Austro-Hungarian Empires in 1918 are too recent to be publicly available. Of those which existed before then, quite a few have had changes of boundaries since the records began, thus, for instance, Danish census records cover what became part of Germany in 1864, and the boundaries of both France and Italy have changed since they began to keep censuses. Modern French returns began in 1836, although there were returns of a sort as much as 200 years earlier. Italian returns date from 1885, and like the French ones, are held in district archives. Danish returns are held centrally, and though beginning in 1787, did not record details such as birthplaces until 1845.

THE FORMAT of census returns is similar everywhere. They are very basic records, almost always on printed government forms, ruled into columns, and under a heading for the place of residence, the columns list names, ages, and all the other particulars of the return in question, and have few, if any, problems of interpretation.

Wills and Probate Records

Wills are invaluable records for genealogists; a man making

his will usually mentions his wife, all his children, perhaps his children's husbands and wives, his grandchildren, possibly brothers and sisters, nieces and nephews, and other friends and relations. He usually identifies where he lived, the property he owns and to which children he is leaving it, and many other personal details. Indeed I have known research cases where a family was so well documented in wills that I have been able to construct a five or six generation pedigree simply from wills, only turning to registers and other vital records afterwards for no greater purpose than to simply fill in the details of dates of birth, marriage and the like on what was already a perfectly good pedigree.

The legal side of wills and probate can become exceedingly complicated, and the following is no more than a summary of the more important points. A person can die either "testate" (leaving a will), or "intestate" (leaving no will), in which case there are complicated rules about division of the inheritance. Moreover, these complicated rules vary from state to state and country to country. A will normally has to be signed by the person making it – the "testator" or, if female, the "testatrix" – and in the presence of witnesses, who also sign. In the past it was quite normal to leave the making of a will until virtually the last moment, on the death-bed. This meant that it was sometimes too late to make a formally written will, and the testator made a verbal or "nuncupative" will, which was declared in front of witnesses and written down afterwards. Minors under the age of 21 could not make wills – although it was possible for a minor's property to be disposed of by the procedures in intestacy. As regards what legacies were made and to whom, this varied, and in different states or countries there were different laws or customs governing the subject. In some places, for example, it was perfectly possible for a testator to leave his property entirely as he wished; in other places, there might be either a legal obligation or even a custom in the district to leave certain proportions of property to different relations. One customary practice in parts of England which was imported into America by some settlers, was that the testator should leave one-third of his property to his widow, one-third to his children, and the remaining third to be disposed of as he wished. Variations continue to this day; in much of the United States, for instance, a child who is disinherited has right of legal redress through the courts but in Canada this only applies in Nova Scotia and not elsewhere. A will normally names one or more executors, who have a legal obligation to carry out the wishes of the testator. In cases of intestacy the court appoints an administrator who disposes of the property according to the local intestacy laws, which usually provide for some formula for division of the property among the relations. The administrator is usually the next of kin – or occasionally a major creditor – and this act by the court is called a "Grant of Letters of Administration" which genealogists usually abbreviate to "*Admon*".

After the testator dies there has to be, by American and British law, a "Grant of Probate" by the appropriate court. This is, briefly, a process of authentication of the will, and an investment of authority in the executor to distribute the property. As a rule, this is a perfectly routine step, and it takes place shortly after the death of the testator. There can, however, be complications; the most usual of these is where the executor named either refuses ("renounces") the task, or is unable to carry it out for some other reason; such reasons could be absence abroad, death, or – perhaps the most common reason of all – that the executor is unable to legally, being under the age of 21. The court then grants "Administration with Will Annexed" (sometimes in abbreviated Latin "*Admon cum test*") to a person who performs the task of an executor. (There

are a great many other complications which can arise; but
they would fill a book of their own.)

PROBATE COURTS are a subject in themselves, but a key one,
because the way most genealogists find wills is by coming
across the copy of it lodged at the court, so you have to know
which court had jurisdiction before you know where to look.
United States probate courts are straightforward, as the
appropriate court is the one for the county, city or district
where the person whose will is concerned lived and died, re-
gardless of whether some of the property left in the will was
outside the territory of that court. So for United States wills,
the general rule is: try the county court-house. Much the same
applied in Canada – apart from Quebec, to which we will
come back later. In England and Wales there was, until
1858, a very complicated hierarchy of probate courts. Briefly,
they were Church Courts (of the Established Church of England) of Archdeacons; above them Bishops; and above them
Archbishops, while the Archbishop of Canterbury's court, the
Prerogative Court of Canterbury claimed superior jurisdiction over all, including — and this is significant for cases con-
nected with emigration from England – overseas. The decisive
factor concerning which court a will was proved in was where
the property was, rather than where the testator died, as the
lower courts had jurisdiction only over limited territories. The
whole subject of English probate courts is so complicated that
people write books and publish maps about them. Anyone concerned is well advised to read these books, but one example
can illustrate how vital it is to know about them. An American
family had traced their ancestors back to a man who died in
the city of Bath, in England, and they had his will which
named his children, including the son who had emigrated to
Philadelphia. The will had been proved in the Bishop of Bris-

tol's court, only about 13 miles away. So the family came over from America every year for their vacation, and searched exhaustively in and around Bath, and they engaged professional researchers to make more searches in and around Bath. This went on for 20 years. I was then engaged to try to solve the problem; the flaw in the research was that Bath was not in the jurisdiction of the Bishops of Bristol, so I knew at once that the man in question had died not owning any property in Bath. Further researches in the Bristol Probate Court uncovered the inventory of the man's property which had been filed at the time of probate of the will. It revealed not only that he lived in Bristol, but the exact street address. One more hour on the probate records resulted in four generations of his pedigree. Two hours work had achieved more than had previously been accomplished in two decades, simply as a result of doing some homework on the probate court jurisdictions.

Scotland and Ireland had similar networks of church probate courts. Those for England and Wales, and for Ireland, were replaced, in 1858, by a government-organized system of local district registries sending duplicates of wills proved up to central national registries in London and Dublin. Scotland was reorganized in 1823.

The legal aspect of wills – and following from that, where to find them – is different in some other countries. The main difference is in those parts of continental Europe where Roman Law applied, as distinct from the Common Law of England, the United States and Canada. In France and Italy, for example, the wills were drawn up and witnessed by "Notaries Public" (local attorneys with a semi-official status); there was no probate procedure in court. The notaries simply keep the wills for a period – often for 100 years – and older ones are sent to the district archives. In Greece, notaries have to send the wills to the court in Athens. In many other countries there

is no official procedure to deal with wills at all – in Scandin-
avia, for instance, there is only a procedure for official distribu-
tion of property between heirs, especially where they were
minors. This does mean that generally these records are difficult, if not impossible, to find, because it is only from the official copies of wills in court records that, in general, we know
about wills at all.

One point which arises out of this is that in Quebec, with its
French background, there are two types of procedure, one relating to the normal probate court; and the other using
notaries, which is on the French pattern, and the wills never
appear in court records, remaining in the hands of the notaries. There are also minor aspects of Roman Law procedure
in the United States in Louisiana and one or two other states
with French or Spanish connections in their past.

THE FORMAT of a will is usually quite straightforward; the testator begins by declaring his or her name, and, normally, their
occupation and where they lived. A prior commitment of the
property towards paying the costs of the funeral and any debts
is also usual, and this may be followed by a desire to be buried
in a specific place – often a clue in itself as people sometimes
want to be buried in their ancestral burying place, somewhere
away from where they lived. Then there is the list of names
and relationships (if any) of the persons to whom something is
left, with the amounts, and also the name of the executor.
Finally, the date and signature of the testator, often with some
sort of declaration as to its being his or her last and true will,
and also the signatures of the witnesses. There is then added
the formal court record – often in Latin in earlier records –
stating the date of probate, and the name of the executor.
Earlier wills are frequently accompanied by an inventory of
the property. It is worth noting that real estate could not be

left in a will in some countries and legal systems.

Grants of administration were themselves very brief, but often accompanied by a "bond"; this was a document by which the administrator, jointly with one or two other people, usually close friends or relations, pledged payment of a sum of money – usually twice the value of the property in question – as security against failing to perform their duties. The genealogical value of this is simply, in practice, the names of the other persons who gave their bond as well, because they were so often relations.

One great advantage of wills and probate records is that there is usually an index to the court records of wills, and this makes it a swift way to locate a surname, provided, of course, that the family were not too poor to leave wills.

IV

Land Deeds

In the United States and Canada, Land Deeds are one of the most valuable record sources for genealogists. The significance of this is largely historical. In Britain and Europe up to 100 years ago, most people were tenants and not owners of the land, farms and houses they occupied. In America and Canada, however, probably the great majority of free white men who reached adulthood owned some real estate, large or small. In addition to this, the deeds are well recorded and this makes them especially useful. The genealogical value of them is not only the first and obvious one of getting a man located – always important, as once you have a man tied down to a place you know in which local records to start looking for the family – but also in the past people passed on their land to their children much more than they do today. One can therefore find the land passing through several generations in the family. Similarly deeds of land would often include references to relationship, particularly when a father deeded land to a son, or to a daughter at her marriage, as a gift.

To understand the deeds we have to first understand the background. There were really two basic types of transaction : first, the transfer of land from the government of the time (British Crown, colonial, state or federal government) to private indi-

---

Map of the United States, with the years they joined the Union

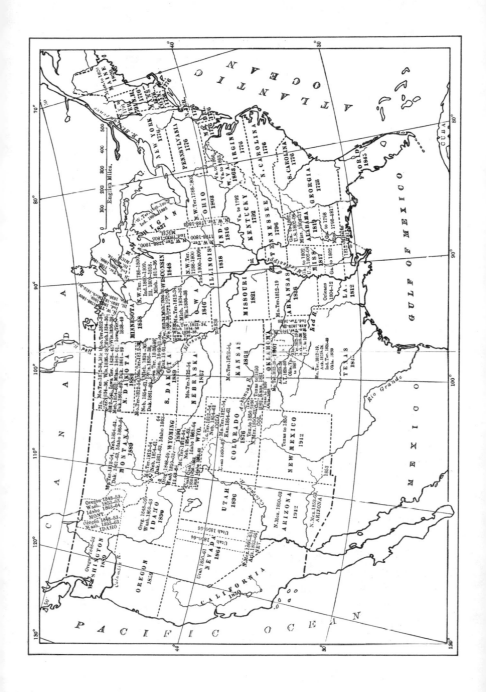

viduals; and, secondly, after this, transfers from one private individual to another.

Government Grants

The first type is – apart from rare exceptions – a government grant of virgin land to a new settler, and the important point about this is that it is always a starting point; it signifies the arrival of a man or a family in a place, and a place where no one else was before him. Either he is a new immigrant or he is a new arrival from elsewhere in America. (The major exception to this was the sale by the states of crown, proprietary and loyalist lands they had seized after the Revolutionary War.)

Before the Revolution these took the form of grants of tracts of land, commonly by "patent", and many of these grants, especially in Virginia, were on the "headright" system, where a person was granted extra land for every person he transported from England. A new type of grant came into use after the Revolution. Congress promised every man who fought in the Revolutionary Army, $50, a suit of clothes and 50 acres of land; many states added to this, and in later wars the idea was continued, usually being called "military bounty land". In addition, non-veterans could obtain land by "cash entry" (*i.e.* they paid for the land), "credit entry" (when they had time to pay), and "donation entry" (when for various reasons, the government wanted to encourage settlement by making free gifts of land). "Homestead entry" was achieved after 1862 by five years residence, and "private land claims" were claims of prior ownership of lands in territories acquired by the United States, such as the Louisiana Purchase of 1803 and lands ceded by Mexico in 1848. The need for these distinctions is not simply fussiness, but because the records in the National Archives are grouped in these classifications, so this is how we find them. Some of these records do give the unexpected genealogical information; for example, the files on each homestead entry case include, for an immigrant, his place of birth and the like.

Private Transactions

The second type of transaction is the transfer of land from one private owner to another. All such transfers were naturally of land which was previously at some time the subject of a government grant of virgin land. As genealogists, our first concern is with where the deed is and how we can find it. Almost all such deeds are recorded in local county or city court-houses, and generally they are indexed by the names of the people involved. Not knowing the county to search in can be rather a problem, which is why we usually have to start our researches in such records as the census. Even the vague and limited information of the 1790 Census can guide you to an actual county, and so to the county court-house with all its treasures. In fact this is a point which comes up time and again in genealogy; most of the useful records are localized ones – deeds registered in one county, baptisms registered in one church, and so on. Without knowing something about where to look, it becomes like looking for a needle in a haystack. Hence the basic sound principle of using generalized sources and records, no matter how vague, to narrow it down. Land ownership maps of many states in the 1800s in the National Archives in Washington are useful in this connection.

Once you have narrowed down your search to one or two counties, there is usually nothing for it but to go to the county court-house and research there. One or two states have started to collect the earlier county court-house records into state archives, and some state archives have microfilm copies of the records in the court-houses, which is a great help.

Title deeds of land can appear large and daunting documents to start with, but when you have read a few of them you come to realize that the bulk of the text of them is routine and almost repetitive legal jargon. One soon learns to pare the facts which need to be noted down to the essentials : the date and the names and descriptions of all the parties to the deed, buyer, seller, trustee, mortgagee – they all matter. Then a summary note of the property, and what is being done; is it being bought and sold, mortgaged, given to a son, or settled on trustees for a daughter at her marriage? Are there any other relevant details, such as the land being described as "lately in the possession of Richard Brown senior, father of Richard Brown junior, the now vendor"? A single sentence like this in a deed can add a generation to your pedigree, and some deeds can add more. Not only does it add to your pedigree but you know that Richard Brown senior was there, at that place, a generation earlier, so you can search back earlier in the same county court-house; if you are fortunate you may build up several generations of the family. In time you will come to a halt. Perhaps it may be that the county in question was one which had been formed by splitting up another county – this often happened in the early stages of settlement – Maine, for example, began its existence as one county only. This may take the search back to another county court-house, or your hunt may have taken you back to the earliest settlement of the area – if nobody lived there previously, you are not going to find any deeds. When you reach this point, you should have arrived at the stage where your ancestor should appear in the original government grants. These will not be in the county court-house but in the state archives or the national archives in Washington. What was he : a soldier granted bounty land or a newly arrived immigrant from Europe, or had he arrived from some other place in America? This is where your researches have to take a new turn.

National Variations

While the great bulk of United States land records are of free-holders owning their own land, several of the colonial period states had extensive tracts of land which were owned by pro-prietors – many of whom were content to sit back in England and simply receive the rents. For these there were, naturally, fewer deeds of ownership in the earlier period, but there are – or should be – rent rolls in the county court-houses which are valu-able lists of tenants. Tenancies were not, however, usually passed down in the families in America – unlike the English ones we mention a little later – so there is not much genealogical informa-tion to be learnt from rent rolls except simply the assurance that a man of that name was there then. Even that, though, is a clue.

In Britain and Europe, there was much more renting of land from a few large landowners – in 1850 90% of English property was rented, and not owned, by the occupiers. This means that deeds of ownership are of much less value, as genealogically they only apply to about 10% of the population. On the other hand the various types of tenancy were often passed down in a family, and contain a great deal of genealogy. However, there are prac-tical problems about the organization of the records, and as a result of this many fewer are available.

In England and Wales there was no official register of deeds. To be strictly accurate, King Henry VIII did bring in a system in 1536, but he made the mistake of also taxing people when they registered deeds, so lawyers invented a type of deed which escaped the rules of the Act as well as the tax. In modern times a land registry has been created, but this came too late to be of much use to genealogists. All title deeds were – and indeed in many cases still are – thus kept by private individuals. This has all the hazards of their being lost or damaged – one can some-times find old English title deeds cut up to make lampshades. Many of them are now coming into county record offices, but it is only a fraction of what must have existed at one time. In Ireland, they did overcome this problem, and there is a Register of Deeds, where title deeds are registered to this day. It begins in 1708 and is very well indexed. This is a particularly valuable feature of Irish genealogical research as so many other Irish records were burnt in 1922 – luckily the Registry of Deeds was in another building. In Scotland, where Roman Law – as distinct from the Common Law of England and most of the United States and Canada, except Quebec – was used, there are registers of "Sasines". These are registers of transfers of possession of land made before Notaries Public, and are in effect a series of registers of transfer of land ownership. Many of the earlier ones are indexed. The amount of reference to tenants in all of these registered records in the British Isles, though, is very limited – they may refer to the tenants by name, but even this is very brief and superficial, and will not give you much genealogy. For information about tenants in the British Isles we have to use other records.

In Denmark, the Land Registry records do include details of tenants, which make them a treasure-house; much the same can be said of Norway and Sweden, although they are less well documented in general. In France and Italy, where Roman Law applied, deeds are kept by Notaries Public apart from some older ones which are in district archives. This principle is fairly general wherever Roman Law was in operation. However, in some countries there were vast areas owned by few people in whose families they continued for centuries, and title deeds are of very little use at all.

In Germany, the situation of the archive sources is complicated by the fact that before the country was unified it comprised literally hundreds of mainly very small states. Each state had its own archives, its own legal system and was independent in every way. APPENDIX B clarifies some of these complexities, but the land tenure system in most of Germany of the period means that tenancy records are of only limited use for genealogists.

Court Rolls and Leases

It was in Britain, where the Common Law applied, together with principles of liberty which eliminated serfdom in the Middle Ages, that tenants had the legal rights behind them which make their records informative. There was one great class of "copyhold" tenants; these had rights of passing on the inheritance of their tenancy, dating back into the Middle Ages. Consequently the court rolls and court books of English manors are a source for genealogy beyond the hopes of what would be possible in most other countries. Briefly, the essential point was that a copyhold tenant's land, on his death, passed to his sons by legal right as next tenants; there were local variations of custom, as to whether it was the eldest son, the youngest son, or all sons equally, but none the less it was inherited. From this, at a later date, grew a system of leasing land for three lives. Basically the way this worked was that a tenant would lease land not for a fixed term of years but for "three lives", *i.e.* the lives of three people named by the tenant – he usually named himself and two sons. This is obviously useful in itself; but what makes it even more useful for genealogy is that the landowners would take great care to record births and deaths of their tenants, and often notes of their ages and ages of those named as "lives" in the leases. If one of the "lives" – that is to say the people named as one of those for whose three lifetimes the lease lasted – emigrated from England, this was also recorded, and sometimes there are in the landowner's archives letters and notes about people in America.

The problem about finding these records, however, is that there is no official registry of leases. They are in the private archives of the landowners, and while some of them have been

deposited in county record offices, many have not – and a considerable amount have probably been lost. After all, there was
no obligation to keep the records when they were no longer useful. The other tricky point about these records of landowners,
whether the leases or the manorial court rolls and court books, is
that if they are in a county record office, they may very well be in
the record office nearest to where the landowner lives, not in the
county they relate to, but possibly hundreds of miles away.

The great value of all land deeds and leases is, to a large extent, in country areas. This is not usually a major problem at the
dates when most genealogists need to use them, as in that early
period people tended to live in the country and farm. The big
cities we know today are mostly creations of the last hundred
years and we are thus dealing with a later period than the dates
which most of us are having to hunt for our ancestors. We can
usually ascertain through our grandparents enough of the history
of our family's last hundred years, so as not to need to do much
research. Moreover, most manorial deeds and court rolls were
no longer in use by then.

V

Other Useful Records

As GENEALOGY is so much involved in the everyday lives of people, and indeed *is* the history of the ordinary people, there are few human activities whose records do not produce some genealogical information about someone somewhere. The difficulty with a book like this one is to know where to stop, because the only real advice anyone can give is never to stop. To select a few of the most useful, however, we have :

Military Records

We have already seen how many land titles date back to military bounty land granted after the Revolution or later wars; in fact, there are two ways – apart from family memory or tradition – in which research is generally led back to military records. One is from the census, not forgetting that the 1840 Census made a special listing of Revolutionary and military pensioners; the other is from tracing the family back in land deeds to a military bounty land grant. It did not, however, start at the Revolution.

THE COLONIAL PERIOD saw very little true peace from the French, Indians or Spaniards at any time up to the Revolution. There are a few listings, rolls, musters and the like, but nothing that one could call a seriously kept official archive. The first bounty lands, however, were granted in the Colonial period, by Virginia, largely land in what is now Kentucky (Kentucky was part of Virginia until 1792).

THE REVOLUTIONARY WAR soldiers were not well recorded to begin with, but a great deal was made good by subsequent applications for pensions and bounty land by them or their widows or heirs. It should be remembered that these widows or heirs could claim the rights to which their deceased husband or father would have been entitled if he had been living. The National Archives in Washington has organized the files very efficiently, and everything relating to one soldier is in one file. When you realize that some claims for pensions or bounty for revolutionary soldiers were being made as long as 60 years afterwards by their heirs – who then had to produce a vast amount of records, affidavits, certificates, and the like to prove their case – you can well imagine that some individual files can contain a vast amount of material.

Similar records exist for members of the United States Army and Navy in extensive series right up to modern times. They also include a good deal on Confederate Forces in the Civil War – although for these there is much more in the individual state archives of the Confederate states. Some military and naval records may be not at the National Archives in Washington, but at the Federal Records Centre at Alexandria, Virginia. The most modern records are not available for public research, and some late 19th century records are in the Military Personnel Record Centre, St Louis, Missouri. The wealth of material, together with the extent of indexing of these records that has been done – which makes them readily researched – is such that if there is the slightest possibility of an ancestor having served in the United States Army, the records should be searched. The search might in any case turn up some unknown relations whose papers could be of value on a collateral line.

BRITISH ARMY AND NAVY records are not so well documented as those for the Revolutionary War soldiers in the United States and are less well indexed; however, they start earlier and cover a far wider range, largely as a result of two factors. First, the British government had been established longer, and, secondly, the world-wide extent of the British Empire in the 18th and 19th centuries made this inevitable. One great advantage of the British records is that details of a soldier's marriage and children born while in the Army are recorded.

The following example illustrates what British Army records are capable of showing. We traced a pedigree back to the birth of a child in the married quarters of an Army barracks in England. From the birth registration of the child, we knew the name, rank and regiment of the father. This led us directly to his Army file. From this we learnt that he had enlisted in England, but his age and exact parish of birth in Scotland were given. We had a description of him : height, colour of eyes and hair, complexion, chest measurement, waist measurement, complete medical record – how many genealogists can dig out that much about an ancestor? To be blunt, though, the reason the British authorities took so much care about descriptions was to make it easier to trace the man if he deserted. As well as his full Army career, we were given the precise date and place – and the bride's name – of his marriage in India, and the birth dates and places of his four children, born in India, South Africa, England and Ireland. In addition, we were told his retirement address, and from his pension papers, we found the date of his death. What would otherwise have called for **week s** of research was all concentrated into one file.

When I began researching the ancestry of British Prime Minister Edward Heath, I understood that his family had always been traditionally linked with Kent, the far south-eastern corner of England. An ancestor had been in the Coastguards,

though, and the Navy records showed that the Heaths had actually originated at the other end of England, in Devon. It was
a posting in the Coastguard service which explained why they
had moved from the opposite corner of the country.

It is always worth remembering that the British Army had
several German regiments. This was so during the Revolutionary period, and although the records at that date are not so
detailed as they were later – such as the ones just mentioned –
they can give a great deal of personal detail about the numerous Germans who, after their discharge – or even after antici-
pating their discharge by deserting – settled in the United States
and Canada.

In other European countries, there are generally extensive
records of conscripts. Unlike the United States and Britain,
most continental European countries had a system of conscrip-
tion; compulsory military service for every young man – or all
of a certain social range – for perhaps two years. This gener-
ated records as officials tried to make sure that everyone liable
for the service did it – that is they kept records so to be able to
identify "draft dodgers". In Denmark, they registered poten-
tial draftees *at birth* from 1788, which is almost as good as
having centralized vital records.

Marriage Licenses

These cause much confusion, because they are quite different
things west and east of the Atlantic, though called the same.
Essentially an American marriage license is issued by the civil,
lay, local government authority – *i.e.* a record of it is usually
filed at the county court-house or city hall, and it is the essential step before a church marriage. The exact procedure varies
from state to state, but the essential point is that marriage
licenses in court-houses and city halls are the primary source
for American marriages.

European marriage licenses were – before modern government vital records – an entirely different thing; they were issued by the church authorities, usually the bishop or his deputy, in special circumstances only. Only a small minority of marriages are covered by such a license.

The normal church marriage in Europe was after the "calling of banns" – which was simply a public announcement on three successive Sundays of the intention of the couple to marry, announced in the home parish churches of both the future bride and bridegroom. The idea was simply to ensure that they were both free to marry and there was no obstacle, such as their being married already, or being too closely related. The "calling of banns" was a medieval procedure which was continued by both the Catholic and, after the Reformation, the Protestant Churches. It was varied in form – for example Quakers made searching enquiries through the Monthly Meeting, and, even for adults, the consent of parents was usually desired. During the few years of the Puritan government in England which set up government vital records instead of church ones, in the 1650s, there was an alternative to announcement in church, by announcing it in the market-place on three successive weekly market days. And much the same happened all over Europe, with local variations.

A European marriage license was a license from the bishop to allow the couple to marry without the formality of calling banns. The reasons for this were usually fairly obvious. The most common reason was for a couple who wanted – or needed – to marry in a hurry, without the three-week delay of calling banns. In addition to the inevitable human reason for this, examples could be of soldiers and sailors who might be posted away in less than three weeks – and in any event would, while on service, not always have a convenient home parish church for banns to be called. People with social pretensions who did not like the idea of their forthcoming marriage being publicly proclaimed also got licenses. The last category was of people whose eligibility to marry was in doubt, such as widows whose widowhood could not be vouched for locally, or were under the age of 21 and had no parents available to give permission.

Bishops would issue marriage licenses only after the future bride and bridegroom had sworn oaths as to their freedom to marry, and frequently had given a bond for a substantial amount of money which would be forfeited if their oath turned out to be false. The affidavits and bonds often survive in diocesan archives, and are full of personal information about the people.

In general, the value of European marriage licenses is that they are a great aid to tracing the "difficult" and elusive marriage. The majority of marriages were by banns, and between brides and bridegrooms who lived quite near to each other. Bishops' licenses help to locate the unexpected ones in the unlikely places.

Other Church Records

One of the great problems about genealogy is when people moved away *to* somewhere unknown, or arrived somewhere *from* an unknown place. This is because so many records we use are local ones. When a person or a family moves, they move out of reach of the records we are working on, and all too often we do not have the faintest idea where they have gone to or come from. In the United States, with its many Churches and denominations, there was the very useful custom of recording arrivals and departures of members of congregations, often giving departing brethren and sisters certificates of membership which they could produce to a new congregation on their arrival in a new place. This was particularly well documented by the Quakers, whose records in all matters are generally without

equal. It is not uncommon to find in a Monthly Meeting minute book agreement to give a certificate to a Friend planning
to move away, and to find in the minute books of the destination Monthly Meeting a record of the Friend's arrival, and
even, if we are lucky, the original certificate. For Friends this
applies even for emigration, and it can be quite a thrill to find a
certificate in the archives of, say, a Meeting in Pennsylvania,
where not only is there a certificate from the immigrant's home
Meeting in England, but the handwriting of the certificate is
identical to the handwriting of the clerk who wrote the minute
book back in England, noting the agreement to issue a certificate to their departing member.

The other type of church record which is often of value is
particularly in the Protestant Episcopal Church. This Church
brought over from England in the early colonial period the
functions which were carried out in England by the church-
wardens and the Overseers of the Poor, who were generally
styled "the Vestry" in America. In particular, there was the
duty of caring for the poor, which we now think of as a government social security matter rather than a Christian duty
towards our neighbours. Briefly, each individual parish would
raise the necessary money locally to look after anyone in misfortune. However as the money to do this was raised in the
parish, there was the rather less Christian attitude that any
recent arrivals who became chargeable to the parish for relief
should be sent back to where they had come from. This was,
of course, a very close procedure, although without legal backing, to the English Poor Law system. In English parish records
the full development of this can be so well documented that
we can often tell more about the poor than about the very rich.
We know exactly what food they were allowed, what clothing,
when and for how much they were given new shoes – we know
all of this for British Prime Minister Edward Heath's ancestors,

even the cost of a Heath funeral and beer for the mourners, paid for by the parish. The most genealogical information comes from the question of "settlement", where they had lived in the past, and which parish or vestry was liable for their support – in English records this can even be a detailed affidavit of their life's history, from birth, through employment, wages earned, where they lived and other details.

This was not, however, something which was exclusive to English or English-type Protestants. Christian charity to those in misfortune can be found, and is documented, in all Churches, whether Catholic, Quaker, Lutheran or Baptist, both in America and in Europe.

Generally documents of this type are found kept with the parish or church registers, in one place. Unfortunately the attention given to publishing and indexing registers has not yet been given to vestry records.

VI

Immigration Records and Research

SOONER OR later all American genealogical research – apart from Indians – is going to come to the water's edge, so to speak, with an ancestor who arrived in North America from "somewhere else", usually somewhere in Europe or perhaps Africa. This is always the "big jump" in your research. It follows from the nature of genealogy. You trace from the known to the unknown, backwards in time, step by step, usually with some sort of continuity of some kind of record, even if it is only a vague one. Now you are faced with your ancestor having arrived from another continent, from somewhere keeping quite different types of record, and all too often without any really firm evidence of where he came from.

One of the lessons which we appreciate in *Debrett's* offices every day is the value of sound "homework" on immigrant research, and how infrequently this has been done properly. Any professional research organization like ours – and perhaps ours more than most, as we have offices both sides of the Atlantic – knows the type of enquiry. A client will come to us with the information: "my great-great-grandfather was William Simpson; he turned up in Delaware in 1866 with a wife and I think he immigrated from Scotland". We ask: "Why do you think Scotland". Answer: "Well, Simpson is a Scottish name isn't it?" To which we have to reply that it is just as much an English name and there are many Simpsons in Ireland. Has he searched the census? No. Shipping lists? No. He has just traced the family back and lost the trail. Simply because people cannot find an ancestor, they jump at immigration as the obvious conclusion.

In fact, immigrant research falls into two main groups. Anyone who arrived in the United States after about 1820 comes into the category where there is a high probability of a record actually stating where the immigrant came from.

Immigrants arriving after about 1820

THE CENSUS should be the first and most basic research tool in this connection. This is covered in detail in CHAPTER III but to summarize the points which relate especially to immigration :

1. Heads of families are named in every census, starting in 1790. A very basic check – so basic that people often do not think of it – is to search earlier census returns, to see if the family were there when you think they might not be. To express it in the simplest terms, if a man was named in the 1790 Census, you know he did *not* immigrate in 1810.

2. Foreigners not naturalized are numbered, but not named, in the Census in 1820 and 1830. It is of course a problem that they are not named, but often the name of the head of the family is a clue. This is always a pointer to searches in local court records for naturalization papers.

3. In every census from 1850 onwards, the state, territory or country of birth, plus the age, is stated.

4. In 1870, the Census recorded whether males over age 21 were US citizens or not.

5. In 1870, the Census also noted whether the mother and father of the person were of foreign birth – which took the immigration question back a generation. An elderly person answering this question in 1870 could well be identifying as foreign-born his parents born as much as 100 years before.

6. In 1880 and 1900, the Census went further and noted the actual birthplaces of both father and mother. This took the retrospective information about the previous generation, first raised in the 1870 Census with a straight "yes" or "no", a stage further with the positive naming of a state or country.

7. Finally, in 1900, the returns record the actual year of immigration into the US. It also recorded the actual month and year of birth.

Quite obviously, the census returns, if used properly and thoroughly, can provide a great mass of information about most immigrants in the 19th century. Naturally there will be some who, by mischance, could have arrived in the United States just after one census, had children born, and then died before the next census; but these will be a small minority. Moreover, where, perhaps, a direct ancestor has missed the census returns for some reason, often a brother or sister can be found whose birthplace supplies the same answer.

THE HOMESTEAD ACT of 1862 is another source. Basically, without going into all the details, this was a grant of a tract of land which became the applicant's property by his farming it for five years. Amongst the qualifications were a statement of name, age and a copy of naturalization proceedings if the applicant was not born a United States citizen. In the case of aliens, a declaration of intention to become a citizen had to include the information of the port and date of arrival and the country of birth. This act continued to be effective until 1908. Land Deeds are discussed in CHAPTER IV, but the fundamental point here is that, if your ancestor acquired homestead land between 1862 and 1908, the file in the National Archives will either show you that he was a United States citizen by birth, or it will tell you – by a copy of his naturalization papers or alternatively by details of his intention to apply for naturalization – of his country of origin.

SHIPS' PASSENGER LISTS (of arrival in America) are the next in importance. While there are quite a number of miscellaneous earlier lists, they originated more or less by chance, but the lists beginning in 1820 are a result of specific legislation. In theory, all passengers arriving at all US ports from 1820 should be recorded with their name, age, sex, occupation and countries of origin and destination. As we learn all too often in genealogy and research, though, the theory of what *should* be in records and what actually *is*, are usually two different things. Some of these lists have gaps in them, perhaps for years or even decades. Even so they are very useful records, and most of them are in the National Archives. A more detailed listing is the Immigration Passenger Lists, of which one port starts in 1883 and most of the others which matter in 1893, from which date they record a great deal of information. This includes, as well as the obvious name, sex, age and marital status, the last residence, destination in the United States and details of any relation the immigrant was going to join. In 1906–7, it was even extended to contain a description, birthplace and the next of kin in the country of origin – for genealogists the regret is only that this was not done at least 100 years earlier.

A great many of these lists have been indexed, especially the earlier ones, in some way or another. For those that have not been indexed, the search can be narrowed down if you can get, from the 1900 census, the date of immigration – and allow for a year or two's margin of error in the date stated.

Full details of these lists and where they are will be found in the source material listed in APPENDIX B.

EMIGRATION PASSENGER LISTS vary greatly, because the passengers came from a wide range of countries, each with their own governments and own systems, whereas the United States at their destination had only one government making the rules. So, for example, in Denmark, Norway and Sweden, the police listed emigrant passengers leaving the country, but in Great Britain it was never government policy. Many British shipping companies did keep lists although without legal obligation. Indeed the major British Atlantic shipping company, the Cunard line, did so, but the British Board of Trade destroyed them all in 1900. Various passenger lists do, however, emerge from time to time – only recently a large collection of lists of Irish passengers to America was found, completely by chance, in a locker in Cork, Ireland, 100 years after the events. France kept lists of emigrants : these are in the Archives Nationales in Paris. Italy attempted to do so, but without much success or value to us, as many Italian immigrants to America left Italy unofficially.

The most important lists are those at Hamburg. This port and Bremen, in Germany, were the two main ports for immigrants to the United States from central and eastern Europe. The Hamburg lists have been microfilmed for the period 1850–1934 and indexed by the LDS Genealogical Department, and for 1850–1873 at the Library of Congress, Washington. Similar lists for Bremen were destroyed by bombing.

NATURALIZATION papers are not so much of a research aid as might be expected, largely because they only became comprehensive at a later date than most people need the information. Basically, prior to 1868, the concept was citizenship of the individual state, not of the nation. Moreover, not all immigrants became naturalized, which did not bar their children born in the United States from citizenship. Most earlier naturalization proceedings are in state courts and are difficult to locate, other than for four states : Maine, Massachusetts, New Hampshire, and Rhode Island, where all naturalizations prior to the new legislation in 1906 have been indexed. The difficulty about many states is that the formalities were often quite casual, and frequently a simple signature to a statement of allegiance was adequate, or even a passenger list was used as a naturalization list. In many cases, the only way that proof of naturalization emerges is if the new citizen applied for either a passport or for homestead land.

THE POLITICAL GEOGRAPHY OF EUROPE is a major problem in locating immigrant ancestors' European origins because of its constant changes. Europe at the time of the great waves of immigration which ended in 1914 was a very different place to what it was to become between 1918 and 1939, not to mention today. Places of birth stated by immigrants in census or immigration records may have ceased to exist as countries, or be something quite different now. Poland, Czechoslovakia and Yugoslavia, for example, did not exist before 1918, and immigrants from those countries might well describe themselves as from Russia, Austria-Hungary, Germany, Serbia or Montenegro. The maps show the frontiers as they were and as they are now.

The advantage of working on more recent immigration is that not only is there better documentation of modern records, shipping lists, census and the like on this side of the Atlantic, but one can connect up with what are usually similar modern-type records east of the Atlantic, in Europe. Even if the immigrant left Europe too early to appear in the modern records himself, probably his brother or even his parents could be found.

Earlier Immigration

Earlier immigration than about 1820 to North America does pose quite big problems when it comes to locating the European origins. On the other hand, there were many fewer of them, and they came from a much more limited area. In fact, before 1820, immigrants to the United States were virtually exclusively from the British Isles or, fewer in total, Germans from in particular the Palatinate (Pfalz) and Hesse. There were also, of course, the

French in Canada. Many of them came from readily definable groups, which makes for aids in narrowing down the field of search – ever the secret of this type of problem. Seeking the British (or German) origins of an early immigrant with nothing to indicate particulars can be another "needle in a haystack" search. The technique should be to progressively narrow down the size of the "haystack" until it reduces the search involved to manageable proportions. This, in my experience, is essential. The initial searches should be in America, to fill out all possible details about the immigrant, his general background, context and associates. Every little detail can provide a clue.

Not least, perhaps, is to be sure, before embarking on extensive – and probably costly – researches in Europe, that the man in question really is an immigrant and has not simply moved in from the next state. It is all too easy to trace a family back until they have clearly "appeared from somewhere else" and fall on the conclusion of immigration; notwithstanding that a family newly appeared in Georgia may not be immigrants at all, but fresh arrivals from the Carolinas or Virginia.

THE QUAKERS are an obvious example of a group that stands out easily. Their records on both sides of the Atlantic are generally as ideal as one could reasonably hope for. In particular, British Friends' records are so superbly and thoroughly indexed and organized that there are as a rule few problems with Quakers compared with other cases. Quakers tend to be found largely in Pennsylvania and Delaware, especially in the 1680s, following William Penn's leadership. They later spread out, though, into Virginia, the Carolinas and elsewhere.

THE "SCOTCH-IRISH", so called, were Presbyterians who came from Northern Ireland. They were descendants of the original Scottish settlers in Ulster and sought new lands because of a

Europe 1914

combination of political unrest in Ireland and population pressure, which started to build up a century after the original "Plantation of Ulster" (early 1600s). The bulk of them went to what was then western Virginia, western North Carolina – the areas which later became Kentucky and Tennessee – and Pennsylvania, spreading out over the Ohio and Mississippi. They are fairly easily recognized, being Presbyterian, and their generally Scottish names are also a useful indicator. Indeed one can be reasonably confident that anyone with a Presbyterian belief and Scottish name, who appears in the areas mentioned in the period

Europe today

between about 1710 and 1770, is almost certainly "Scotch-Irish". This narrows down their British origin to six or eight counties in the north of Ireland. Here, however, is a classic trap for searchers; Ireland today is divided on a primarily sectarian basis, the six counties of Northern Ireland being predominantly Presbyterian/Protestant, as distinct from the predominantly Catholic south. It is a popular fallacy to think of the Scotch-Irish as coming from exclusively the present-day political Northern Ireland, whereas for research purposes the frontier and consequental split in some archives is artificial and misleading. There were substantial numbers of Presbyterians beyond this frontier in, for example, counties Donegal and Monaghan.

The problems of the genealogy of the Scotch-Irish are rather more a matter of the problems of Irish records than anything else.

THE EARLY PURITANS OF NEW ENGLAND have a significance which is in danger of being lost amidst the over-emphasis placed on some aspects of immigration. There is no doubt that the Pilgrim Fathers went to Plymouth first and foremost for liberty of worship, but there are signs that this was not the exclusive reason for some of those who followed them. It is not generally realized that the fishermen of the south-west counties of England knew and fished the east coast of America from the Grand Banks of Newfoundland all the way down to the Carolinas long before there was any permanent settlement. Men of Devon, in England, were making a great deal of money out of Newfoundland codfish 70 and 80 years before the Pilgrim Fathers landed. There is some evidence that men of Bristol were fishing there before Columbus; a letter to him from Bristol – now in the Spanish archives – may be proof that they told Columbus about the new land across the ocean. What is quite certain is that the part played by west-country Englishmen in American history has been under-estimated. It was, after all, at Exeter in Devon that the Massachusetts Bay Company had its headquarters; it was in a Devon manuscript that the very phrase "New England' was first written down; and the American word "fall", for what most Englishmen call "autumn", is simply the Devon dialect that they use to this day. It is also true that statistically there were more puritans in Devon and Somerset, two adjoining counties, than anywhere else in England and also statistically true that the port of Barnstaple in Devon had more ships sailing from it than did London. We could argue whether they were puritans first or fishermen first, but more probably it was a bit of each. The lesson is therefore to think about *why* men emigrated from a settled and prosperous society to the New (but hazardous) World. The reason will often help the research.

To religious freedom, and economic opportunity of new fishing grounds, can be added political freedom. Robert Parker, a typical Virginia "cavalier" settler took advantage of this political freedom; and his case illustrates a point that is often forgotten – people could, and did, come back to England again, as easily as they went. Here is the original entry in an English country parish register; it refers to the civil war in England (when the Puritan Parliamentarians defeated the Royalist Cavaliers) :

Robert Parker . . . [*and*] Jane Baxter . . . maried the 3 daye of Jully 1650 & happening to be of the Kings partie was forsed to fflie, that yeere went into Virginia in regard of the warr & lived thear 8 yeeres with his wife, returned 1658. Abegall Parker was borne the 3d Jully 1651. George Parker the eldest sonn Borne the 10th of Aprill 1653. Margarett Parker Born the 26th of September 1655 . . . George Parker sonne of ye above said Robt Parker was Married to Joan Green . . . [*in England*]

Thus we have a generation of a family born in Virginia, but the earlier and later generations resident in England. Robert Parker had two brothers who continued to live in Virginia. Robert died, in 1673, owning land in Virginia, although he had not lived there since 1658. Interestingly enough, he left it to whichever of his children would go out to live there; one of his daughters did so, and married a Virginian. This shows that much early immigration was not simply "one way".

VII

Putting It All Together

Types of Pedigree

THERE ARE basically three types of pedigree or ways of drawing up your ancestry in a chart. The first is the one we show for the Greenwood family; this is the conventional rectilinear chart for a single surname family, but with branches. The second is the same type of material, *i.e.* a single-surname family, but in the form of a narrative pedigree; we illustrate part of the Buxton entry in an old edition of *Burke's Peerage and Baronetage*. Thirdly, there is the "all lines" pedigree chart of Amelia Joy Barrett.

They are all equally valid; but you have to ask yourself at quite an early stage of your researches which is the type that interests you. The real question is whether you want to follow up only one line of your ancestry or try to follow up all lines. The "all lines" approach does certainly have its merits, but the problem does arise that you double up the number of lines you are following with each generation : 4 grandparents, 8 great-grandparents, 16 great-great-grandparents; and so on, 32, 64, 128 – 12 generations means over 2,000 ancestral lines. To research each of these lines, beyond a certain point, is hardly a practical proposition. The rectilinear chart type is clear and easily read; but it does have practical problems of space, especially for publication. The narrative form is without equal for publication purposes, but can lose clarity if too much is put into one pedigree.

The choice is really one which will suit your objective. I do

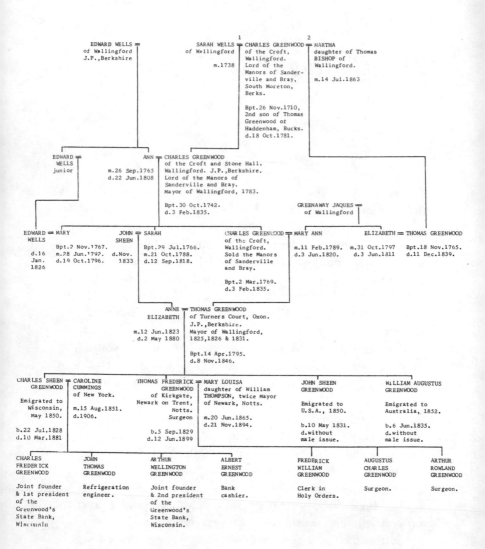

The Greenwood family tree: conventional rectilinear chart

Lineage—The family of Buxton can be traced for the last three centuries in the parish of Coggeshall, Essex.
William Buxton, of Great Coggeshall, Essex, was buried there **22** Dec. 1625, leaving, by Anne his wife, a son,
Thomas Buxton, of Great Coggeshall, *bapt.* there 3 July, 1608, *m.* 1636, Susan Sudbury and *d.* in 1646, leaving a son,
Thomas Buxton, of Great Coggeshall, *bapt.* 19 Oct. 1643 ; *m.* 1668, Judith Gunton, and *d.* 16 Oct. 1713, leaving a son,
Isaac Buxton, of Great Coggeshall, *m.* Elizabeth Arwaker, and had (with three daus.) six sons, **1.** Thomas, of Great Coggeshall, who *m.* thrice, and *d.* in 1777, leaving issue ; **2.** Isaac, *d.s.p.* in 1766 ; **3.** John, of Great Coggeshall, who *m.* twice, and *d.* in 1751, leaving issue ; **4.** Charles, of whom presently ; **5.** William ; **6.** Samuel, of Great Coggeshall, *d.s.p.* in 1757. The 4th son,
Charles Buxton, of Braxted, Essex, *b.* 5 Feb. 1703-4 ; *m.* 29 Feb. 1727-8, Hannah, dau. of George Read, citizen of London, and had issue,
1. George, sometime of Chelmsford, and afterwards of Greenwich, M.D., F.R.S., *b.* 14 Dec. 1730 ; *m.* 18 Jan. 1758, Maria, dau. of John Chandler, of London ; and *d.s.p.* 1 Jan. 1805.
2. Isaac, of whom presently.
1. Elizabeth, *m.* 1752, Samuel Enderby, of London.
2. Hannah, *d. unm.* in 1780.
3. Mary, *m.* 1762, William Hood, of Bardon Park.
The 2nd son,
Isaac Buxton, of Bellfield, Dorset, *b.* 22 Jan. 1733 ; *m.* 5 March, 1755, Sarah, only dau. of Thomas Fowell, and had (with a dau., Sarah, *m.* in 1777, Charles Dumbleton, of Horsley, near Epsom) two sons, **Thomas Fowell**, his heir ; and Charles, who *m.* Hannah, dau. of Samuel Enderby. The elder son,
Thomas Fowell Buxton, of Earl's Colne, Essex, high sheriff of that co., *b.* 1 Sept. 1756 ; *m.* 12 Feb. 1782, Anna, eldest dau. of Osgood Hanbury, of The Grange, Coggeshall, Essex, and *d.* 3 Dec. 1793, having had issue,
1. Thomas Fowell (Sir), 1st bart.
2. Charles, *b.* 16 Dec. 1787 ; *m.* 19 Dec. 1811, Martha, eldest dau. of Edmund Henning, of Melcombe Regis, Dorset ; and *d.* 4 July, 1817, having had issue,
  Edmund Charles, of Daresbury Hall, Warrington, and Buxton House, Essex, *b.* 2 Sept. 1813 ; *m.* 3 Sept. 1834, Charlotte Mary, eldest dau. of Abbot Upcher, of Sheringham, Norfolk, and *d.* 1876, leaving by her (who *d.* 16 Nov 1892) issue,
  (1) Edmund Charles, of Coed Derw, Bettws-y-Coed, co. Carnarvon, J.P., *b.* 24 Jan. 1839 ; *m.* 1873, Gertrude, dau. of Richard Sykes, of Edgeley, Cheshire.
  (1) Anna Mary.   (2) Augusta Charlotte.
  (3) Catherine Emma, *m.* Rev. W. T. Vale.
Anna, *m.* 15 July, 1836, Joseph Hoare, 4th son of Samuel Hoare, of Hampstead ; and *d.s.p.* 19 July, 1840. (*See* Hoare, Bart., *of Sidestrand*.)
3. Edward North, *b.* 22 April, 1791 ; *d.* 25 Aug. 1811.
1. Anna, *m.* 3 Oct. 1816, William Forster, of Bradpole. He *d.* 27 Jan. 1854, leaving issue.
2. Sarah Maria, *d. unm.* 18 Aug. 1839.
The eldest son,
Sir Thomas Fowell Buxton, 1st Bart. of Bellfield and Runton, *b.* 7 April, 1786 ; *m.* 13 May, 1807, Hannah, 5th dau. of John Gurney, of Earlham in Norfolk and by her (who *d.* 30 March, 1872) had issue,
1. Edward North (Sir), 2nd bart.
2. Thomas Fowell, of Easneye, Ware, Herts, and Upton House, Cromer, J.P., Herts, high sheriff 1878, M.A. Camb., *b.* 29 Aug. 1821 ; *m.* 5 Feb. 1845, Rachel Jane, 5th dau. of Samuel Gurney, of Ham House, Essex (*see* Burke's *Landed Gentry*). She *d.* 6 Jan. 1905. He *d.* 27 Jan. 1908, leaving issue,
  1 ♦ John Henry, of Easneye, Ware, Herts, and Upton House, Cromer, M.A. Camb., D.L., high sheriff co. Herts 1897 (*New University Club*), *b.* 15 Aug. 1840 ; *m.* 19 Nov. 1874, ♦ Emma Maria, dau. of Capt. Edward Wilson Pelly, R.N. (*see* Pelly, Bart.), and has issue,
    (1) ♦ Henry Fowell, B.A. Camb. (*Groves Manor, Sawbridgeworth*), *b.* 23 Jan. 1876 ; *m.* 24 July, 1900, ♦ Katharine Tayspel, dau. of Right Hon. James Round, P.C., M.P., of Birch Hall (*see* Burke's *Landed Gentry*), and has issue,
    1a ♦ John Fowell, *b.* 21 June, 1902.
    2a ♦ Robert James, *b.* 29 April, 1908.
    3a ♦ Joseph Gurney Fowell, *b.* 5 July, 1913.
    4a ♦ Michael Auriol, *b.* 4 Sept. 1914.
    (2) ♦ Leonard (Rev.), M.A. Oxford, Rector of Sheldon, Birmingham, from 1914, *b.* 10 Oct. 1877 ; *m.* 27 July, 1903, ♦ Kathleen Lydia, dau. of the late Capt. John Digby Wingfield-Digby, of Sherborne Castle, and has issue,
    1a ♦ Edmund Digby, *b.* 1 March, 1908.
    2a ♦ Kenneth Leonard, *b.* 19 July, 1909.
    3a ♦ Daniel Richard, *b.* 4 March, 1912.
    1a ♦ Kathleen Hannah, *b.* 6 Nov. 1905.
    2a ♦ Ruth Lydia, *b.* 2 Oct. 1906.
    (3) ♦ Andrew Richard, B.A. Camb., *b.* 19 Aug. 1879.
    (4) ♦ Arthur (Rev.), M.A. Camb., Vicar of All Saint's, Southport, from 1914, *b.* 7 Aug. 1882 ; *m.* 14 Jan. 1908, ♦ Esmé Caroline, 2nd dau. of Francis W. Pixley, F.S.A., J.P., of Wooburn Green, Bucks, and has issue,
    1a ♦ Nigel Arthur, *b.* 28 Jan. 1909.
    1a ♦ Richenda Dorothy, *b.* 30 Nov. 1911.
    2a ♦ Mary, *b.* 10 June, 1913.

(1) ♦ Dorothy Rachel ; *m.* 14 July, 1903, Sir Arthur Grey Hazlerigg, 13th bart., and has issue.
(2) ♦ Margaret Katharine, *m.* 9 July, 1912, Rev. Edward Louis Longfield McClintock, Vicar of Haltwhistle, Northumberland, son of Lieut.-Col. C. E. McClintock, of Glendaragh, co. Antrim, and has issue (*see* Burke's *Landed Gentry*).
(3) ♦ Lilian Rosamond.
2. Arthur Fowell (Rev.), *b.* 21 Feb. 1851 ; *d.* 31 July, 1881.
3 ♦ Geoffrey Charles, of Dunston Hall, Norwich, J.P. and D.L., Norfolk, vice-chairman of Norfolk Terr. Force Association, D.L. Norwich, sheriff 1890, mayor of Norwich 1903, late maj. and hon. lieut.-col. Norfolk Yeo., formerly lieut.-col. 1st vol. batt. Norfolk Regt. (V.D.) (*Oxford and Cambridge, and Brooks' Clubs*), *b.* 21 June, 1852 ; *m.* 3 Sept. 1878, ♦ Mary, eldest dau. of Hon. and Rev. John Harbord (*see* Suffield, B.), and has issue,
  (1) ♦ Geoffrey Charles, major R. Riding of Yorks Yeo., late Norfolk Yeo., *b.* 4 June, 1879 ; *m.* 9 April, 1902, ♦ Clare Florence Mary (from whom he obtained a divorce, 1913), only child of the late Sir Francis George Stapleton, 8th bart., and has issue,
    ♦ Peter Stapleton, *b.* 14 Oct. 1904.
  (2) ♦ Bernard, Lieut. Comm. R.N. (*Castor, Peterborough*), *b.* 21 Oct. 1882 ; *m.* 28 Sept. 1904, ♦ Lady Hermione Grimston, 2nd dau. of 3rd Earl of Verulam, and has issue,
    1a ♦ Geoffrey Mungo, *b.* 26 May, 1906.
    2a ♦ Simon Fowell, *b.* 22 Nov. 1908.
    3a ♦ Samuel Luckyn, *b.* 10 March, 1914.
    ♦ Janet Hermione, *b.* 6 Jan. 1913.
  (3) ♦ Ivor, capt. (from whom Norfolk Yeo., B.A. Camb., *b.* 28 Aug. 1884.
  (4) Guy, *b.* 19 Jan. 1888, *d. unm.* 1 July, 1907.
  (1) ♦ Joan, *b.* 8 April, 1881, *m.* 15 May, 1901, Sir John Frecheville Ramsden, 6th Bart., and has issue.
  (2) ♦ Olive, *b.* 3 May, 1886 ; *m.* 11 Sept. 1904, Major Miles Roland Charles Rawlinson, D.S.O., 4th son of Sir Jonathan Backhouse, Bart., and has issue (*see that title*).
  (3) ♦ Avery, *b.* 3 July, 1889 ; *m.* 22 May, 1911, Hon. Guy Greville Wilson, M.P., D.S.O., 2nd son of Baron Nunburnholme, and has issue.
  (4) ♦ Hazel Mary, *b.* 19 Jan. 1893 ; *m.* 10 Aug. 1914, Capt. W. St. George Clowes, late 10th Hussars.
  (5) ♦ Rose, *b.* 25 Feb. 1898.
4 ♦ Alfred Fowell, of Fairhill, Tonbridge, B.A. Camb., Alderman London C.C. (*Athenæum Club*), *b.* 28 March, 1854 ; *m.* 6 Jan. 1885, ♦ Violet, dau. of Very Rev. Thomas William Jex-Blake, D.D., of Bunwell, Norfolk, and has issue,
  (1) ♦ Patrick Alfred, *b.* 24 March, 1892.
  (2) ♦ Denis Alfred Jex, *b.* 26 April, 1895.
  (1) ♦ Violet Elizabeth, *b.* 13 Feb. 1900.
5 ♦ Barclay Fowell (Rev.), of Kobe, Japan, M.A. Camb., honorary missionary in Japan, *b.* 16 Aug. 1860 ; *m.* 22 July, 1888, ♦ Margaret Morris Amelia, dau. of William Railton, of 65, Onslow Square, S.W., and has issue,
  (1) ♦ Murray Barclay, *b.* 30 July, 1889.
  (2) ♦ Alfred Barclay, *b.* 3 Nov. 1891.
  (3) ♦ George Barclay, *b.* 16 Oct. 1892.
  (4) ♦ Barclay Godfrey, *b.* 7 Jan. 1895.
  (1) ♦ Rachel Jane, *b.* 11 June, 1905.
  1 ♦ Rachel Louisa.
  2 ♦ Elizabeth Ellen, *m.* 12 Feb. 1888, Robert Barclay, of High Leigh, Hoddesdon, Herts, and has issue.
  3 ♦ Catherine Emily, *m.* 9 Sept. 1891, Thomas Morris MacKnight, who *d.* April, 1906.
4. Margaret Jane, *m.* 26 April, 1882, Rev. Canon R. A. Pelly, vicar of West Ham, Essex. She *d.* 28 Nov. 1903, leaving issue (*see* Pelly, Bart.).
5 ♦ Effie Priscilla, *m.* 1 Aug. 1893, Rev. Thomas Lancaster, Rector of Melcombe Regis, Weymouth, and has issue.
6 ♦ Ethel Mary.
3. Charles, of Foxwarren, Cobham, M.P. for East Surrey, *b.* 18 Nov. 1822 ; *m.* 7 Feb. 1850, Emily Mary, eldest dau. of Sir Henry Holland, 1st Bart. (*see* Knutsford, B.). She *d.* 19 June, 1909. He *d.* 10 Aug. 1871, leaving issue.
  1 ♦ Fowell Henry (*Oxford and Cambridge and City Liberal Clubs*), *b.* 31 July, 1852.
  2 ♦ Sydney Charles, created Viscount Buxton (*see that title*).
  1 ♦ Eleanor Margaret (*Scat Manor, Woking*), *m.* 7 Sept. 1877, Cecil William Boyle, and has issue (*see* Cork, E.). He was killed in action in South Africa, 8 April, 1900.
  2 ♦ Mary Emma (74, *Eaton Square, S.W.*), *m.* 27 Oct. 1887, Albert Osliff Rutson, and by him (who *d.* 21 April, 1890) has issue.
3 ♦ Richenda, *m.* 3 Jan. 1907, Hon. Reginald Gilbert Murray Talbot, 2nd son of James, 4th Lord Talbot of Malahide.
4 ♦ Sybil de Gournay, *m.* 16 Aug. 1887, George Stapylton Barnes, C.B., of Fox Holm, Cobham, Surrey, eld. son of late George Carnac Barnes, J.P., and has issue.
1. Priscilla, *m.* 1 Aug. 1834, Andrew Johnston, of Renny Hill, M.P., and *d.* 24 Aug. 1852. She *d.* 18 June, 1852, leaving issue.
2. Richenda, *m.* Captain Philip Hamond, of Annesley Park, Notts, and *d.* 15 June, 1858, leaving issue.
This gentleman having distinguished himself by his philanthropic exertions to abolish slavery, was created a baronet 30 July, 1840. He *d.* 19 Feb. 1845, and was *s.* by his eldest son,
Sir Edward North Buxton, 2nd Bart. M.P., *b.* 16 Sept. 1812 ; *m.* 12 April, 1836, Catherine, 2nd dau. of Samuel Gurney, of Upton, Essex, and by her (who *d.* 18 Aug. 1911, aged 97) had issue,
1. Thomas Fowell (Sir), 3rd bart.
2. Samuel Gurney, of Catton Hall, Norfolk, J.P. and D.L., sheriff, 1891, *b.* 1 Nov. 1838 ; *m.* 18 Sept. 1861, Louisa Caroline, youngest dau. of the late John Gurney Hoare, and by her (who *d.* 1 March, 1879) had issue,

16 RICHARD ALLAM
Farmer

8 RICHARD ALLAM
Publican/Master Wheelwright
BORN 13 September 1840
WHERE Islip, Oxon.
DIED 30 November 1871
WHEN MARRIED
WHERE HARRIET

17 RACHEL PERRY

18 JAMES COLWELL, Hurdle maker

4 RICHARD ALLAM
BORN 27 September 1872
WHERE Stanton St. John
WHEN MARRIED 14 October 1895
DIED 14 November 1919
WHERE Islip, Oxon.

9 HARRIET
BORN 28 November 1839
WHERE Stanton St. John
DIED 14 February 1913
WHERE Hemel Hempstead

19 EMMA GOODWIN

20 THOMAS BLACK, gentleman

2 AUBREY ALLAM
BORN 12 April 1902
WHERE Kirtlington, Oxon.
WHEN MARRIED 1 November 1930
DIED 23 April 1977
WHERE Beech Cottage,
Bradley,
Hampshire.

Of Ashe Warren, Overton,
butcher (1932); of Lower
Wield, publican and Pest
Officer for Hampshire.
Gamekeeper (1951)

5 ADELA CLARA
BORN 3 March 1870
WHERE Fawley, Hampshire
DIED 9 February 1965
WHERE Lymington,
Hampshire.

10 TOM BLACK, yeoman
BORN circa 1820
WHERE Finchley, Middlx.
WHEN MARRIED 11 June 1862
DIED 1891, Fawley
WHERE

21 CATHERINE RENDALL

22 JAMES FLEMING, Yeoman

11 JANE MARY
BORN 4 July 1836
WHERE Godshill Isle of Wight
DIED 1934, Stockwell
WHERE Surrey

23 MATILDA FANNY URRY

24 NATHANIEL SMITH, agricultural Lab.

1

AMELIA JOY
BORN 20 August 1932
WHERE Ashe, Hampshire
WHEN MARRIED
DIED
WHERE

NAME OF HUSBAND OR WIFE

EDWARD JOHN ARTHUR
BARRETT

3 FREDERICA WILHELMINA
BORN 7 May 1909
WHERE Overton, Hampshire
DIED
WHERE

Housekeeper (1930)
Gamekeeper

6 EDWIN JOHN SMITH
BORN 8 March 1873
WHERE Overton
WHEN MARRIED They didn't !
DIED 11 October 1952
WHERE Royal South Hants
Hospital, Southampton

12 WILLIAM SMITH
BORN 12 March 1840
WHERE Overton
WHEN MARRIED 18 August 1864
DIED 9 March 1911
WHERE ANNE

25 LUCY HUTCHINGS

26 ROBERT BLACKBURN, agricultural Lab.

13 ANNE
BORN 12 February 1843
WHERE Overton
DIED
WHERE

27 JANE RAMPTON

28 EDWARD LOVELL, baker

7 MARIA
BORN 4 May 1873
WHERE Overton
DIED 1942
WHERE Wield

R.A. (1900)
Grocer (1909)
Kennel Huntsman (1930)

Servant (1900)

14 HENRY GEORGE BROWN
BORN 19 January 1838
WHERE Andover Workhouse
WHEN MARRIED 3 April 1867
DIED ? 1907
WHERE MARY (twin)

29 MARIA BROWN

30 No. 26

15 MARY (twin)
BORN 12 February 1843
WHERE
DIED 18 June 1926
WHERE

31 No. 27

recommend, though, if you choose the narrative pattern, that when actually doing the research you use the rectilinear chart type, and then postpone preparing the narrative text until after you have completed the research. The point of this is that when you are engaged in the actual research, the extra clarity of the rectilinear chart is beneficial.

Source References and Research Methods

The first step in research will be to write up all the information which you have gathered from the family. It is always important to include, as far as possible, all names, dates, and places – a name without dates can in many cases be meaningless, and dates of events without places equally so. This is simply because they cannot be verified. All research results should be capable of being verified and the information given in a form that identifies its source. For example, an entry "William Brown born 1842", without anything else, is worthless; but "William Brown, baptized 24 April 1842 at Valley Springs Presbyterian Church, West Virginia" is much better. You now know where the family were living and could discover which county Valley Springs lay in. Then you could go to the county court-house and work on deeds, or pick up the family in a census. Furthermore it means that this is information which is verifiable – simply by searching the registers of baptisms at that church. Similarly, a reference to a will should include the date of probate and the probate court. Any other piece of information should have the additional items which make it verifiable. This gives your research authority and confidence.

You will probably have material on your grandparents, and perhaps one or two earlier generations, from family knowledge. For the earliest generation on the pedigree, you will most prob-

---

"All lines" pedigree chart of Amelia Joy Barrett (née *Allam*)

ably have the age at death, but no precise details of birth or baptism – remembering that the two are interchangeable for our purposes, indeed you may well have no option, as baptism records generally exist earlier than birth records. In any event, you should be able to find the family in the indexed 1900 Census which will give you the information of ages and places which, put together on your chart, will fit each other like the pieces of a jig-saw puzzle. Each item will lead you on to the next one – the age at death leads to a birth record; the birth record leads to a marriage record; the marriage leads back to two more birth records, and so we can go on back.

It can happen, of course, that birth records do not exist, and it is here that we turn to other records. Wills are an obvious choice. Say we have traced back to a Henry Brown who we know was married and having children in Valley Springs, Virginia, in the 1780s. There are, however, no baptism registers of the church before 1780. We also know that the 1790 Census shows two other Brown households nearby, so it looks as if he has relations in the area – and that usually means a family settled there for a generation or two. A search in the county court-house produces a will of Henry Brown senior; he mentions "my son Henry Brown junior' and, perhaps, "my grandchildren, sons and daughters of my son Henry Brown junior". He names them, and their names agree with what you already know of Henry Brown junior's children . . . "It fits". This is just as good as a specific baptism or birth record; it is documented proof that Henry Brown junior was son of Henry Brown senior. In genealogy, this is what we need; proof of relationship is the point, not proof of precise dates of birth. It is quite as good to have an entry in the pedigree "mentioned in his father's will 1787 proved Cornwall county". It might be a will, it might be a deed of land, or other documents, but the exact source is immaterial; what matters is the information. One point which does need to be mentioned, because it is invariably overlooked, is that of wills of relations of other surnames. Wills – and other documents too – of the wife's family, and of, for example, married sisters and aunts, can all help. It is a point which can double the information available, if it is remembered.

It is naturally impossible to elaborate upon every permutation of problems and evidence available, and more effective to give the sources available, explaining some general principles of approach, and how to use the information.

Finding More about Where They Lived

One of the most fascinating extensions of "pure genealogy" can be to take the researches further, into finding just where the family lived, to perhaps identifying the church where they worshipped, even to reading the wills they wrote in their own handwriting. It makes the "names on bits of paper" far more like real people if you can give them a genuine context.

In the later census returns, a precise address and location of residence is no problem, but for the early census, the groupings of the returns are vaguer. You cannot say "it was this place". Deeds are, of course, essential for this. Some deeds may be very precise in identifying a piece of land; some may include maps or plans; they may relate to landmarks, rivers, creeks or roadways, which enable you to identify the actual place.

A problem about this, in colonial America, was the lack of building materials. Most houses were built of wood in the early colonial period, and those that did not burn down by accident were often burnt down deliberately to recover the nails. So do not expect to find the actual house where your ancestors lived, though you can probably find the place to within a few hundred yards. It is well worth the extra research involved as it gives an extra dimension to your researches.

In Europe, there is usually a better chance of success in getting your family pinpointed to a place. In the first place, there were more records. Taxation lists can often help, because they were usually made out by someone walking round the town or village always following the same route. Thus each building came in the list in a certain order, year after year – in Winchester, for instance, the city tax was assessed in the same order for 400 years.

Also in Europe, there was much more use of brick and stone for building. This means that far more buildings of the period have survived, including the churches. These were where your ancestors were actually baptized or married, and outside in the churchyard is where they were buried – you may even find their memorials.

A further way in which you can become personally involved with your ancestors is in European archives. Most wills and deeds in American court-houses are not the originals, but copies of them entered into registers. The bulk of the English probate court records, however, are the actual original documents which the testator signed personally. So are many deeds. To see these is quite thrilling and it does give your ancestors so much more of a real context in English history.

APPENDIX A

Heraldry and Coats of Arms

THERE IS a considerable amount of misunderstanding about this subject. In the first place, a "Crest" is no more than a part of the "Achievement", and is not properly separate. The raven arising out of a ducal coronet shown in the Washington Arms is the crest. The other great fallacy is the belief that there is such a thing as a correct Coat of Arms for a surname in general. It is entirely wrong to believe that *anyone* of a given surname is entitled to a certain Coat of Arms, and the commercial practice of selling reproductions of Coats of Arms alleged to "belong to a name" is technically quite wrong. The Law of Arms is that correct and lawful entitlement to Arms is acquired either by specific grant from the proper authority, or by inheritance from someone who has previously been granted those Arms. The law varies slightly from country to country, but the basic point is that, as a rule, Arms can only be inherited in the male line – usually all male lines of descent – and they can only pass through the female line if the woman in question is an "heraldic heiress".

Thus George Washington's Arms, shown here on his bookplate were his by inheritance from his male line Washington ancestors. The only other men entitled to use those arms would be *only* those Washingtons who descended from the same original Arms-bearing man; *not* all Washingtons.

It is often said that the Stars and Stripes derive from the Washington Arms. This is certainly possible, but it is unproven.

George Washington's armorial bookplate
(Courtesy, Mr Peter Drummond-Murray)

What is certain, however, is that the flag of the District of Columbia, with three red stars and two red stripes on a white background, *is* the Washington Arms.

APPENDIX B
Reference Sources

THE REAL key to research and getting results is knowing what record to look for and, then, where to find it. This chapter is basically a guide to where to find the records. It does not claim to be a final and complete list but aims to be a short practical one, which includes guides to more comprehensive lists you can use as you learn more about the subject.

North America
United States

GENERAL SOURCES

It is absolutely essential to get the geography right; so much of genealogy is related to jurisdictions of churches and governments, and unless you know the right areas, you will not find the right records :

Atlas of American History, James Truslow Adams (New York, 1943).

Columbia-Lippincott Gazetteer of the World (New York, 1952).

The Counties of the United States and their Genealogical Value, E. Kay Kirkham (Salt Lake City, 1965).

Libraries are so vital that you have to know where they are :

International Library Directory, A. P. Wales (London; biennial)

American Library Directory (New York; biennial)

GENEALOGICAL REFERENCE BOOKS

The three most complete reference sources to genealogies already published are :

Genealogies in the Library of Congress, Marion J. Kaminkow (Baltimore, 1972).

The Genealogical Index (Newberry Library, Chicago) (Boston, 1960).

American and British Genealogy and Heraldry, P. William Filby (Chicago, 1970).

The standard guides to American newspapers are :

History and Bibliography of American Newspapers 1690–1820 Clarence Saunders Brigham (Hamden, Conn, 1962).

American Newspapers 1821–1936; a Union List of Files Available in the United States and Canada, Winifred Gregory (New York, 1937).

Directory of Historical Societies and Agents in the United States and Canada, Donna McDonald (Nashville, Tenn; biennial). Standard guide and address list of all the societies and organizations in North America, and an indispensable guide for finding local societies.

A Bibliography of Ship Passenger Lists 1538–1825, Lancour and Wolfe (New York, 1963). The only guide to lists in the early phases of American settlement. After 1825 the main and most complete series survive in the National Archives.

The Researcher's Guide to American Genealogy, Val D. Greenwood (Baltimore, 1975). Probably the most comprehensive guide to research available.

VITAL RECORDS AND REGISTERS

There are four standard guides to vital records in the modern period (although of limited value for earlier dates) :

Where to write for Birth and Death Records, United States and Outlying Areas (Public Health Service Publication 630A–1)

(US Government Printing Office; revised periodically).

Where to write for Births and Deaths of US Citizens who were Born or Died Outside of the United States and Outlying Areas (Public Health Service Publication 630A–2) (US Government Printing Office; revised periodically).

Where to Write for Marriage Records, United States and Outlying Areas (Public Health Service Publication 630B) (US Government Printing Office; revised periodically).

Where to Write for Divorce Records, United States and Outlying Areas (Public Health Service Publication 630C) (US Government Printing Office; revised periodically).

WPA List of Vital Statistical Records (Works Projects Administration, 1943). Catalogues the lists made by 40 states of their existing and known vital records and registers in the late 1930s and early 1940s.

NATIONAL ARCHIVES

Guide to Genealogical Records in the National Archives, Meredith B. Colket, Jr and Frank E. Bridgers (National Archives, Washington, 1964). The most comprehensive guide; includes the best guide to military records.

The National Archives have published a series of pamphlets on the census returns; the primary one is:

Preliminary Inventory of the Records of the Bureau of the Census, Katherine H. Davidson and Charlotte M. Ashby (National Archives, Washington, 1964).

CHURCH ARCHIVES

American Baptist Historical Society, 110 South Goodman Street, Rochester, NY 14620.

American Catholic Historical Association, Catholic University of America, Washington, DC 20017.

Church of Jesus Christ of Latter Day Saints, Genealogical

Department, 50 East North Temple Street, Salt Lake City,
Utah 84150.

Congregational Christian Historical Society, 14 Beacon Street,
Boston, Massachusetts 02108.

Greek Orthodox Archdiocese of North America (Archives of),
10 East 79th Street, New York, NY 10021.

Lutheran Ministerium of Pennsylvania Historical Society,
Lutheran Theological Seminary, 7333 Germantown Avenue,
Philadelphia, Pennsylvania 19119.

Mennonite Historical Society, Bluffton College, Bluffton, Ohio
45817.

Moravian Archives, North Main at Elizabeth, Bethlehem,
Pennsylvania 18015.

Mother Church, First Church of Christ Scientist (Archives of),
107 Falmouth Street, Boston, Massachusetts 02110.

Presbyterian and Reformed Church Historical Foundation,
Assembly Drive, Montreat, North Carolina 28757.

Protestant Episcopal Church Historical Society, 606 Rathervue
Place, Austin, Texas 78700.

PROFESSIONAL RESEARCHERS

Board for Certification of Genealogists, 1307 New Hampshire
Avenue North West, Washington, DC 20036, publishes a list
of certified genealogists in the United States and Canada.

Debrett Ancestry Research, Suite 303 East, 200 Park Avenue,
New York, NY 10017, offers a professional research service
in both North America and Europe.

Canada

[N.B. Four million Canadians have immigrated to the United
States]

GENERAL SOURCES [*see* under UNITED STATES]

GENEALOGICAL REFERENCE BOOKS

Tracing your Ancestors in Canada (Queen's Printer and Controller of Stationery, Ottawa, 1967). A government pamphlet and a useful first guide.

Searching for your Ancestors in Canada, Eunice Ruiter Baker (Ottawa, 1976). Includes a very full list of addresses of archives, societies, etc.

Directory of Historical Societies and Agents in the United States and Canada, Donna McDonald (Nashville, Tenn, 1975). [*see* also under UNITED STATES]

ARCHIVES [*see* also under BRITISH ISLES and FRANCE for the Colonial Period]

There are two World Conference on Records (Salt Lake City, 1969) seminar papers:

Records of Genealogical Interest in the Public Archives of Canada, James J. Atherton.

Church Records of Canada, Margaret Meikleham, Glenn Lucas, T. R. Millman, Francois Beaudin and Erich Schultz.

PROFESSIONAL GENEALOGISTS [*see* under UNITED STATES; both addresses given also cover Canada]

Mexico

The only reference book in English on Mexican genealogy is *LDS Research Paper H/2*. All records are in Spanish, Latin or in Indian dialects. A great deal has been microfilmed by the LDS (Mormon) Genealogical Department. It is important to remember that Mexico was a Spanish colony and there are extensive archives relating to Mexico in the *Archivo de Indias*, Seville, Spain.

SOCIETY

Academia Mexicana de Genealogía y Heráldica, Mexico City, has a large collection of genealogies, biographies, etc.

ARCHIVES

Archivo General de la Nación, Palacio Naciónal, Mexico City 2, has holdings which include land, tax, etc, records from 1524. Mexican Indian records from the year 900 – copies available at Brigham Young University, Provo, Utah. [Most military records before 1700 are in Spain (*see above*).] Immigration records 1820–1850 are here (for other years *see below*). There is a census of Spaniards only 1689 (for modern census *see below*).

La Casa Amarilla, Mexico City, holds census returns of great detail, beginning 1842.

Archivo Histórico de Hacienda, Mexico City, holds immigration records 1519–1820.

Archivo des Ex-Ayuna-Miento, Mexico City, holds immigration records from 1917.

US Immigration and Naturalization Office, El Paso, Texas 79984, has records of immigrants to the United States from Mexico since 1903.

VITAL RECORDS AND REGISTERS

Parish priests in individual parishes hold parish registers, some beginning as early as 1524.

Civil Registrars in each district hold modern vital records of birth, marriage, and death since 1859.

PROFESSIONAL GENEALOGISTS [*see* under UNITED STATES]

British Isles

Ethnically, Americans are about 50% British, and about 82% of Americans have at least one British ancestral line. This means that the British Isles are far and away the most important area outside America for American genealogy. The degree of union between the various countries which comprise the British Isles has varied at different dates, and this affects where the records are. For example, Irish military and similar records before 1921 are in London, England, in the government archives there.

England and Wales, Channel Islands, Isle of Man

Wales was conquered by the English in the Middle Ages and politically united with England in 1542. There may be some political separation in the near future, but it is not clear what, if any, effect this will have on the location of archives. The Welsh speak a language of their own, but this is used only to a limited extent in the records most genealogists will meet with, and it is only necessary to learn a few words. The Established Church is the (Protestant Episcopalian) Church of England. The Church in Wales has been separate in organization since 1914, but this is of very little significance to genealogists. At periods when the Established Church is relevant to genealogists, other Churches were in a small minority.

The Channel Islands and Isle of Man both have slightly anomalous status, as, while under the British Crown, they are not part of the United Kingdom. Their archives are largely, but not entirely separate (*e.g.* Channel Islands census records are in London, but none of their vital records are there). The listings which follow include them.

GENERAL SOURCES
Survey Gazetteer of the British Isles (Bartholomew's) (Edin-

burgh; regularly revised). The standard Gazetteer for all of the British Isles.

Ordnance Survey Maps are government-published maps in a wide variety of scales and formats, covering all of the British Isles (catalogue from Ordnance Survey, Southampton, England).

The Institute of Heraldic and Genealogical Studies, Northgate, Canterbury, Kent, England, publish maps specially designed for genealogists, in counties or groups of counties, showing individual parishes, and also the jurisdictions of probate courts. These cover England and Wales only.

International Library Directory, A. P. Wales (London; biennial).

GENEALOGICAL REFERENCE BOOKS

Federation of Family History Societies Handbook (by post from 2 Stella Grove, Tollerton, Nottingham, England; revised annually) lists almost all genealogically and heraldically interested societies in the British Isles, from the prestigious Society of Genealogists, 37 Harrington Gardens, London, SW7, to small local groups.

The two standard bibliographies of published British genealogies are :

The Genealogist's Guide, George W. Marshall (London, 1973).

A Genealogical Guide, J. B. Whitmore (London, 1953).

Burke's Family Index, Hugh Montgomery-Massingberd (ed) (London, 1976). An index to genealogies published by the company since 1826.

Tracing Your Ancestors (British Tourist Authority, 680 Fifth Avenue, New York, NY 10019). A free leaflet sent to postal enquiries.

In Search of Ancestry, Gerald Hamilton-Edwards (Chichester, 1974). The best beginner's guide to English genealogy; includes a very useful list of other books.

In Search of Army Ancestry, Gerald Hamilton-Edwards (Chichester, 1977). The standard guide on British military records.

ARCHIVES (INCLUDING REGISTERS AND VITAL RECORDS)

Abstract of Arrangements Respecting Registration of Births Marriages and Deaths in the UK and other countries of the British Commonwealth and in the Irish Republic (Her Majesty's Stationery Office, London, 1952). A detailed guide to civil registration of vital records since 1837 in England and Wales, and at other dates elsewhere.

Record Repositories in Great Britain – Royal Commission on Historical Manuscripts (Her Majesty's Stationery Office, London, England; revised regularly). The standard official list of archives of all types including county record offices, throughout Great Britain, Northern Ireland, the Isle of Man and Channel Islands. [*Not* the Irish Republic.] This includes lists of repositories of vital records and parish registers. Many of those listed publish guides and/or lists of their holdings.

Original Parish Registers in Record Offices and Libraries (1974) and *First Supplement* (1976) (by post from Local Population Studies, Tawney House, Matlock, Derbyshire, England). A valuable guide to location of many parish registers.

National Index of Parish Registers (Society of Genealogists, London; in progress). A projected 12 volume guide to all parish registers in Great Britain. Four volumes of introduction and text have been published, and one listing parish registers (of six South Midlands and Welsh Border counties) to date.

Parish Register Copies, Parts I and II (Society of Genealogists, 1977). Lists of copies of parish registers in the library of the society and elsewhere.

Parish and Vital Records Listings (Salt Lake City, Utah, 1977; revised regularly). The guide to the Computer File Index (CFI) of the collections of the Genealogical Department of the Church of Jesus Christ of Latter Day Saints.

There are two guides on the intricacies of probate courts throughout the British Isles:

Wills and Their Whereabouts, Anthony J. Camp (privately published by the author, 162 Westbourne Grove, London W11, England, 1974).

Wills and Where to Find Them, J. S. W. Gibson (Chichester, 1974). Includes maps.

PROFESSIONAL GENEALOGISTS

The following are able to undertake research:

The College of Arms, Queen Victoria Street, London EC4V 4BT.

The Society of Genealogists, 37 Harrington Gardens, London SW7 4JX.

Association of Genealogists and Record Agents, 123 West End Road, Ruislip, Middlesex HA4 6JS, England, supplies a list of freelance genealogists, including members of various leading companies in the profession.

Debrett Ancestry Research, Parchment Street, Winchester SO23 8AT, England, is the research division of an old company in the genealogy business since 1769, with offices and agents all over the world.

Scotland

Scotland was independent from England during the Middle Ages. From 1603 the two countries had one ruler, but separate government. The two countries were united by the Act of Union of 1707, but retained many separate features, including the legal system and courts. It is likely that there will be some political separation from England in the near future, but this is unlikely to have any significance concerning the location of archives. The Established Church is the (Presbyterian) Church of Scotland. There is also the (unestablished) Protestant Episcopal Church, the Roman Catholic Church – strong in the remoter islands of the north-west, where the Protestant Reformation never reached – and the Free Church, which broke away from the Established Church.

GENERAL SOURCES [*see* also under ENGLAND AND WALES]
There are no parish maps published at present but it is worth enquiring from *Miss Susan Moore*, East Lodge, Newliston, Kirk-liston, West Lothian, Scotland, who is planning to publish some.

GENEALOGICAL REFERENCE BOOKS [*see* also under ENGLAND AND WALES]
In Search of Scottish Ancestry, Gerald Hamilton-Edwards (London, 1972). The best book on the subject; includes very useful book lists and other guides as well.

ARCHIVES (INCLUDING REGISTERS AND VITAL RECORDS) [*see* also under ENGLAND AND WALES]
Scottish archives are unique in that a vast amount is collected in-to two buildings close to each other. In England, for instance, this material is scattered among numerous county record offices. The Scottish archives include civil registration of vital records begin-ning in 1855 and *all* Church of Scotland parish registers up to that date or later. The census, probate, and taxation records are also in the same two buildings. There is no current list or guide published, the last listing of Old Parochial Registers having been made in 1872 and the last *Guide* published in 1905. Scottish Census returns are identical in date and type to English ones but more recent ones, up to 1891, are available to the public.

PROFESSIONAL GENEALOGISTS [*see* also under ENGLAND AND WALES]

The Lord Lyon King of Arms, New Register House, Edinburgh, Scotland, will undertake research and has exclusive jurisdiction over Scottish heraldry.

Miss Susan Moore, East Lodge, Newliston, Kirkliston, West Lothian, Scotland.

Ireland

Ireland was a separate kingdom, but ruled by the Kings and Queens of England. Until 1800, it was semi-independent and had its own Parliament, but was then united with England. Finally, in 1921, the larger, southern part was formed into the Irish Free State (later the Republic of Ireland), independent of England. But six north-western counties in the province of Ulster chose to remain, as Northern Ireland, part of the United Kingdom. The Established Church was the (Protestant Episcopalian) Church of Ireland, but only a minority of the population were members of it. In the south, the very great majority were Catholic; and in the north, Presbyterian. The history of Ireland's government has had a considerable effect on the archives, and their location. Certain types of records, such as military records, created before 1921, are in English archives in London. Many more local records relating to what is now the politically separated Northern Ireland before 1921 are in Dublin, in the Republic. The following listing does not distinguish the modern political divisions of Ireland, because so far as genealogy before 1921 is concerned, they did not exist. If we followed any other course, research would only become confused.

GENERAL SOURCES [*see* also under ENGLAND AND WALES]

Handbook on Irish Genealogy (Dublin, 1976) [*see below*], includes genealogical maps of Ireland.

GENEALOGICAL REFERENCE BOOKS [*see* also under ENGLAND AND WALES]

A Simple Guide to Irish Genealogy, Rev Wallace G. Clare and Rosemary ffolliott (London, 1966). A sound basic guide to the subject.

Burke's Irish Family Records, American Edition, Hugh Montgomery-Massingberd (ed) (New York, 1976). The good general introductory section is also published separately (as *Burke's Introduction to Irish Ancestry*).

Handbook on Irish Genealogy (Dublin, 1976). By far the best reference work and guide; it includes valuable maps, lists of existing parish registers, and other lists. Indispensable for Irish research.

ARCHIVES [*see* also under ENGLAND AND WALES]

There is no comprehensive official guide to Irish archives and their holdings; the *Handbook on Irish Genealogy* does, however, include an excellent summary of these. The essential fact about Irish genealogical research is that a considerable amount – but not so much as many pessimists think – of Irish records were lost by fire in the Four Courts Building in 1922. About half the parish registers of Ireland went, and a great deal of the probate records. Irish census records 1813 to 1851 were, apart from a few fragments, also lost in that fire. The Census for 1861 to 1891, inclusive, were not kept by the government. Returns for 1901 and 1911 are available in the *Public Record Office*, Dublin. Civil registration of vital records began in 1864, apart from Protestant marriages, which were registered from 1845 onwards. These records were not destroyed in the fire of 1922. Almost all surviving parish registers in the Republic are still in the custody of the parish priests and ministers. An important and often under-used source is the *Registry of Deeds*, which has recorded almost every land deed since 1708, and thus is of as much importance to Irish research as are the county court-houses of the United States for American research.

PROFESSIONAL GENEALOGISTS [*see* also under ENGLAND AND WALES]

The Chief Herald of Ireland, Dublin Castle, Dublin, Republic of Ireland, undertakes research.

The Ulster-Scot Historical Foundation, Law Courts Building 66 Balmoral Avenue, Belfast, Northern Ireland, will undertake research with particular interest in "Scotch-Irish" immigrants in the United States.

Jews

Jewish genealogy is a subject in itself. First, it has no links with any specific country, in so far that Jews moved from country to country much more than most races, and they had little national tie with their country of residence. Secondly, the Christian Church records which are such a major source for most European and North American genealogy are simply irrelevant.

GENEALOGICAL REFERENCE BOOKS

Finding Our Fathers, a Guidebook to Jewish Genealogy, Dan Rottenberg (New York, 1977). The most comprehensive guide to the subject in print.

In addition, reference should be made to sources for national archives under the headings of the various countries.

ARCHIVES

Central Archives for the History of the Jewish People, Sprinzak Building, Hebrew University, PO Box 1149, Jerusalem, Israel, has the largest collection of Jewish archives. Holdings include vast microfilm collections of Jewish archives of which the originals are elsewhere. Also a great treasure; although the Nazis in Germany destroyed many Jewish registers and records, and even tombstones, their systematic thoroughness was such that they meticulously photocopied or recorded everything before they destroyed it. Happily the Jewish records from Germany survive in this way, and the Nazi records are all now in Jerusalem. The Central Archives also hold catalogues of many Jewish records elsewhere in the world.

These four organizations all hold Jewish genealogical archives; most are written in Hebrew or Yiddish :

Jewish National and University Library, Hebrew University, Jerusalem.

Yad Vashem, Har Hazikaron, Jerusalem.

Sephardi Community Archives, Hahavazelet Street, Jerusalem.

Diaspora Research Institute, Tel Aviv University, Tel Aviv.

American Jewish Archives, Clifton Avenue, Cincinnati, Ohio. This is the largest collection of Jewish archives for the entire North and South American continents, and has outstanding indexes.

There are other very extensive collections of records in numerous other libraries and archives in the United States. A full descriptive list is given in *Finding Our Fathers (see above)*. In addition, refer to the various national archives.

Continental Europe

The first point which has to be made about research in Continental Europe is that the records are written in the native language of the country, or – especially for Catholic records – in Latin. Many German and other north European countries, in the earlier periods – about the 18th century and before – used the Gothic script, which is difficult for the unpractised to read. In eastern Europe, the Cyrillic and Greek alphabets were used. Without knowledge of these, any attempt at personal research is simply a waste of time; the cost of travel would be better spent on engaging a professional. Secondly, you must take into account all the practical consequences of changes in political boundaries which have occurred in mainland Europe since the great immigration period of 80 to 90 years ago. Some entire countries which exist now did not exist then, and vice versa. This makes the location of archives very complicated, and the following is only a brief summary.

In general, most European governments began to keep vital records and census returns in the middle of the 19th century, though this tended to be earlier in north and western Europe than in the south and east.

Austria

Archives comprise the *National Archives* in Vienna – which also include records of the former Austro-Hungarian Empire, relating to many parts of Europe beyond the present frontiers of what is today a small country – and provincial archives in each "land". For a guide see *LDS Research Paper C/16* "Major Genealogical Sources in Austria"; also *C/18* "The Austro-Hungarian Empire Boundary Changes and Their Effect". There is a society of genealogists: *Heraldische-Genealogische Gesellschaft*, Haarhof 41, A-1010, Wien, Austria.

Belgium

Belgium as such did not exist before 1831; prior to this it had a varied history having been Spanish, Austrian, French and Dutch. Government vital records date from 1796. Earlier parish registers start from, as a rule, the 17th century, with a few before 1600 and one before 1500. The LDS Genealogical Department has microfilmed all Belgian parish registers; a copy is in Utah and another in the *Archives Generales du Royaume*, 78 Galerie Ravensteen, Bruxelles, Belgium. A gen-

ealogical society in Belgium is *Office Genealogique et Herald-
ique de Belgique*, Musees Royaux d'Art et d'Histoire, Parc du
Cinquantenaire, 1040 Bruxelles, Belgium.

Bulgaria

This country is fraught with genealogical research problems.
Government vital records began in 1893; earlier church registers reputedly began only in 1860. More recent records are
held by the *District Councils*, earlier ones by the *Ministry of
Justice*, Sofia, Bulgaria. Wills are kept by notaries public (*see*
CHAPTER IV). The government is at present very unforthcom-
ing as regards research. It should be remembered that for a
long period prior to 1878, Bulgaria was a province of the
Turkish Empire.

Czechoslovakia

This country was created in 1918 out of provinces of the Aus-
ro-Hungarian Empire. It is now Communist-governed, but is
the only Communist government in Europe to co-operate readily with genealogical enquiries. Postal enquiries should be
made in the first instance to the *Consular Division, Czecho-
slovak Embassy*, 3900 Linnean Avenue NW, Washington
DC 20008 (or other Embassies in other countries). The
Embassy also issues a free leaflet *Information on Securing
Family History from Czechoslovakia*. Fees are charged for research and reports are written in Czech.

Useful reference sources are: *Ceskoslovensky Vojensky Atlas*
(Prague, 1965), a very detailed atlas; and *Die Deutschen in
der Tschechoslowakei* (Prague, 1964), a valuable guide to
change of place-names from German to Czech after 1918.
There are *State Archives* in Prague; and Czech ones in Prague
and Slovak ones in Bratislava.

Denmark

The Danish Embassy, 3200 Whitehaven Street NW, Washington, DC 20008, issues a free leaflet *Tracing your Danish Ancestors and Relatives*. There is also *The Genealogical Guidebook and Atlas of Denmark* by Frank Smith and Finn A. Thomsen (Salt Lake City), which is a very full guide to Danish records and local geography. The Danish Census began in 1787 and a fully detailed census was first made in 1845. Parish registers began, generally speaking, in about the 1660s. *LDS Research Papers D/5* to *D/10* cover various aspects of Danish genealogical research. There are extensive microfilms of original Danish records in the LDS Genealogical Department Library. Denmark lost territory to Germany in 1864 and regained most of it in 1920 – this complicates research in that area.

Finland

Finland was, until 1918-20, part of Russia, and without any separate government. Hence many archives relating to Finland are in Russia. However local records such as parish registers and the like survive in Finland. The genealogical society of Finland is: *Suomen Sukututkimusseura*, Snellmaninkatu 9-11 00170 Helsinki 17, Finland. The relevant publication is *LDS Research Paper D/4* "Major Research Sources in Finland".

France

France has suffered few major changes of political frontiers at any date relevant to this book. Some parts of far eastern France have been German for a time and, equally, some parts of far western Germany have been French in the past. Belgium has been French and the Italian-French frontier has changed a little. French records are in general well preserved but scattered and hard to locate. French government vital records began in 1792, but these may be in the municipality records or in the district (*départemental*) archives. Parish registers began in parts of France well before 1500, although only a few have survived. They were made compulsory by an ordinance of 1579. After 1667 duplicate registers were kept, much like English Bishop's Transcripts. Following reorganization in 1792, these should be in the *mairies* and *archives départementales*, but like so many records of this type elsewhere in the world, all that should be, is not. Older land deeds and wills are in the district archives, but more recent ones are still held by local notaries public. The census returns beginning in 1836 (and some much earlier) are also in the district archives. The National Archives in Paris hold military records from about 1600. For guides, there is in English *LDS Research Paper G/1* "Major Genealogical Record Sources in France". Much more detailed, but in French, are: *A la Recherche de vos Ancêtres, Guide du Généalogiste Amateur* by Yann Grandeau; and a new guide to genealogical sources in the National Archives (full title and author not yet known), to be published soon. French archives include material relating to colonial period French Canada.

Germany

Germany is important for American genealogy, as after the British Isles, it is the country which makes the largest ethnic contribution to the population of the United States. It is however, a country whose political history makes research tortuous and exceedingly difficult. Politically, Germany was united in 1871, from 39 states, recently reduced to 25.

This number of 39 was itself a major reduction from 100 or more which there had been a century earlier. In so far that it is governments who create archives, the archives of Germany are

Germany: Political Frontiers 1870

chaotic, as each constituent state had its own records. There are the following pamphlets as primary guides: *How to find my German Ancestors and Relatives* by Dr Heinz F. Friederichs (Degener & Co, Neustadt, West Germany, 1969) includes a good summary, and the addresses of 52 State Archives, 86 Town Archives, and 27 genealogical societies. (The sheer numbers reflect the complexities.) There are also *LDS Research Papers C/1* "Major Genealogical Record Sources in Germany", *C/4* "Boundary Changes of the Former German Empire and their Effect upon Genealogical Research", *C/29* "German Church

Records" and *C/30* "Hamburg Passenger List" (emigration records). Another useful reference source is the *Encyclopedia of German-American Genealogical Research* by Clifford Neal Smith and Anna Piszczan-Czaja Smith (R. R. Bowker Company, 1180 Avenue of the Americas, New York, NY 11306).

Today there are yet more political differences; there is the Federal Republic ("West Germany"); there is the Communist-controlled German Democratic Republic ("East Germany"); and there are the former German territories now absorbed into Poland. Many Germans today think of the latter as "East Germany" and so the genealogical society – based in the west – which is concerned with these areas is titled *"ostdeutscher"*, while the area of the German Democratic Republic (DDR) is thought of by Germans as "Middle Germany" and so the appropriate society is titled *"mitteldeutsche"*.

Government vital records are (naturally) as varied as the political past. In those parts of Germany west of the Rhine which were incorporated into the French Republic for some years in the 1790s, a French-pattern registration system was started, and continued after the French left. Here there are registrations of births, marriages, and deaths at the mayor's offices in each town beginning in 1796. In Baden, they began in 1810, followed by Württemberg, Hesse and Frankfurt. The then kingdom of Prussia began in 1874, and the entire German Empire had a unified system from 1876.

Church registers follow the general pattern of western Europe. There are quite a number which start in the 1540–1600 period and the variations of what has survived is much as is to be expected. In brief, a fair element of luck is involved. While increasing numbers of parish registers are being transferred into state archives – and those west of the Rhine are already in the appropriate mayor's office – the majority are still in the individual parishes. As elsewhere, wills, deeds, and such things as enrolments of burghers – which often note birthplaces – can add to the basic information from registers. The great problem about German archives, though, is not so much their survival, as finding them.

This is because the archives, like most archives in the world, relate to the administration which created them – a principle which everyone should always bear in mind. It follows on naturally from the fact that archives are records created not for the fun of it, but for administration of either a church or a civil government. The larger and more organization-conscious German states such as Saxony and Württemberg had better archives, which started earlier and flourished. For some of the smaller principalities, the former rulers still retain the archives of their one-time kingdom in their present residences; some of them are not as well organized or cared for as they might be. Of the parts of Germany now absorbed by Poland, the archives of East Prussia are almost entirely in the west – in West Berlin – but for most of Silesia, the archives remain in Poland.

The secret of good research in Germany is to do very good and thorough "homework". An immigrant to the United States or Canada of German origins needs, first of all, to have every item of information combed through, both in immigration and naturalization papers, and emigration papers in the two German ports of Hamburg and Bremen – from which virtually every emigrant sailed. Religious denominations are also important. In short, one should find every possible clue to narrow the search down to a specific place. Then you have to read up the history of that actual place : who ruled it when, and, as a result, whose archives record the ancestors? Next, what can sometimes be the most frustrating task of all, where are those archives?

One point worth remembering is that a great many of the earlier – and hardest to trace – German immigrants to the United States broke their journey in English ports, especially –

goodness knows why, except that it is a good anchorage – at Cowes in the Isle of Wight. They appear in the records there, and one finds German couples who married there, for example, described in the registers "Palatines bound for Georgia" or similar comments. I have seen as many as 10 German couples' marriages registered on a single page of an English port parish register.

Greece

Greek history is noted for its turbulence. For a long time it was governed by Turkey, winning its independence in the 1830s. Government vital records began in some parts in the 1850s, but it took another 100 years for this to become comprehensive. There are good parish registers, and more recent wills are all filed on the death of the testator in the one court in Athens. In general, research in Greece is hampered by lack of centralization of records and, indeed, paucity of what there is.

Hungary

Hungary was a semi-autonomous part of the Austro-Hungarian Empire. Prior to 1918, its boundaries extended into parts of what are today Yugoslavia, Rumania, Poland and parts of Russia. Government vital records began in 1895. The government then called in all the church registers – including Jews. This was unusual, as most European governments of the time either pretended Jews did not exist or, if they recognized their existence, did so in a less than charitable way.

The National Archives (*Magyar Orzágos Levéltár*, H-1014 Budapest 1, Bécsikapu tér 4, Hungary) hold vital records from 1895 onwards, but only for places within the *present* boundaries of Hungary. Postal enquiries are answered for these but the National Archives staff will not undertake research beyond supplying such certified copies of entries. The National Archives also hold – available for personal research but not for postal enquiries – the church registers up to 1895, mentioned above. Many of these date back to the 18th century. These are from all places within the boundaries of Hungary as they were in 1895 – *i.e.* *including* parts of present-day Yugoslavia, Rumania, Poland and Russia. These latter have all been microfilmed by the LDS Genealogical Department, and are therefore available outside Hungary.

In addition to the National Archives named above, there are 22 provincial archives. The two-volume *Hungarian Library Directory* (Budapest, 1965) lists all libraries and archives in the country.

Before the 18th century, Hungary suffered from invasions by the Turks and a long period of being "fought over"; few early records survived this period.

Iceland

Iceland has all the factors which make for good preservation of records: a small population, isolated on an island, politically stable for a long time and with a long traditional interest in genealogy. There are good records which in many cases can tie up with the earlier traditional pedigrees, leading back to the Viking sagas. The address for all enquiries about Icelandic genealogy is *Ætt- og mannfrædifelagid*, Reykjavik, Iceland. There is a guide in English, *LDS Research Paper D/2*, "Major Genealogical Record Sources in Iceland".

Italy

Italy is another European country which is politically a modern creation. It was formed by uniting a number of states, some of them quite tiny. As a country it dates from 1869, with further territory gained from Austria-Hungary after 1918. Government vital records start in 1869, and before that date parish registers exist but frequently are not as well cared-for as they might be, being very rarely in any archives. There is not any national census, as such things are normally understood, but a similar record on a local basis is the Anagrafe, a series of these having been made from 1885. There is the National Archives in Rome, *Archivio Centrale della Stato*, Corso Rinnascimento 40, Rome, and eight other regional state archives. There are also other archives of municipalities and former states, in a confusing series. This is comparable to the situation in Germany, for much the same reason; Italy being a modern country formed by uniting many smaller but older ones.

As with Germany, the essential need is to get the family you are researching pinpointed to a place. Often, once this is achieved, research can be focused narrowly on that locality and its records, and a fair amount can be achieved.

LDS Research Paper G/2 deals with sources in Italy. *The Instituto Italiano di Cultura*, 686 Park Avenue, New York, NY 10021, includes members with genealogical interests.

Luxembourg

Luxembourg has had a particularly checkered political history, having been at times part of France, the Netherlands and Germany. Government vital records began on the French pattern in 1796, with – at least in theory – all parish registers called into the *mairie*. In short, parish registers and vital records are in very much the same situation as in France, Belgium and Germany west of the Rhine. Other archives are partly in the Netherlands, partly – but to no large extent – in France and in Germany, although wills and land deeds are held locally, again on the French basis in general.

There is no guide to Luxembourg archives published in English. The state archives are directed by Professor Spang, who is also a prominent member of the leading historical/genealogical society : *M le Professeur Paul Spang*, Directeur des Archives de l'Etat, Case postale 6, Luxembourg, Grand Duchy of Luxembourg.

The Netherlands

The Netherlands is almost unique, having a genealogical research organization which is supported by the government. *The Centraal Bureau voor Genealogie*, Nassaulaan 18, The Hague, The Netherlands, is maintained largely by the Ministry of Culture, Recreation and Social Welfare. It has brought together a large proportion of the state and private archives into one place, with very extensive card indexing, microfilming of relevant records in France, Germany, the Dutch colonies and elsewhere. The bulk of the archives brought together are of government vital records, which began in the Netherlands in 1811 (1796 in the far southern provinces) under French conquest, and was set up on the French pattern. Parish registers may need local researches, although there are – in addition to the Centraal Bureau – the state archives, *Algemeen Ryksarchief*, at present at 7 Bleijenburg, The Hague, and 10 provincial archives. It is planned to move the Centraal Bureau to rooms in the new Ryksarchief building in 1979, which will be a useful consolidation. The Centraal Bureau has published a guide in English *Searching for your Ancestors in the Netherlands*. There is a major series of *LDS Research Papers* on the Netherlands : *C/3, C/5-15, C/20-28* and *C/32*.

One interesting addition to genealogy which is possible from Dutch sources is the *Iconographic Bureau*, Sophialaan 9, The Hague, Netherlands. They have there an enormous card index of portraits, photographic negatives, engravings and the like, which aims to collect together portraits of all Dutch people. There is therefore more chance of a Dutch pedigree being illustrated with portraits than most nationalities.

Norway

Norwegian Embassies and Tourist Offices distribute a free but very informative leaflet *How to Trace your Ancestors in Norway*. This is so well drawn up – it even includes tables of population statistics and graphs of emigration patterns – and obtaining this should be the first step in any Norwegian research program.

Census returns are available between 1769 and 1900, of which the return in 1801 is the only really detailed early one. It is only from 1865 that details such as birthplaces are given. Parish priests or ministers fulfilled a double duty by making parish registers also the government registry of vital records. All registers over 80 years old are kept in the regional archives, of which there are seven – all listed in the leaflet referred to. Amongst a great deal of other records, extensive lists of emigrants with personal details have been kept since the late 1860s. These should embrace the bulk of Norwegian immigrants into the United States, as most left Norway after that time. They were Police records; in many of the smaller places they are still at the police stations, although the larger town records are in the regional archives.

Norway was ruled for five centuries by first Denmark and then Sweden, becoming independent in 1905. This means that archives of governmental type to be found in many other countries are not to be found in Norway, as they are in either Stockholm or in Copenhagen. Most of the record-keeping systems are closely paralleled in those two countries. Norwegian vital statistics, for example, are organized almost precisely along the lines of those in Sweden. Nothwithstanding the past history, the wealth of local archives in Norway makes prospects for research here quite hopeful.

Poland

Poland poses many problems of research, largely arising from the combined effects of its history and geography. The ancient kingdom of Poland was partitioned between Prussia (*i.e.* Germany), Austria-Hungary and Russia in the period 1772–95. It was not restored to independence until 1918. This means that for the great period of immigration of Poles into the United States there was officially no such country; they were identified in their immigration and naturalization papers as from Germany, Russia or Austria-Hungary. Then there is the further complication that Poland, as it was restored in 1918, was conquered – by Germany and Russia, again – in 1939. The country as restored in 1945 has substantially different frontiers from what they were in the period 1918–39. A large area of the latter is now included in Russia; a large area of Germany, including much of former Prussia, is now included in Poland. (The last mentioned is the area referred to as "*ostdeutsche*" in relation to German archives – *see above.*) Since 1772, therefore, any reference to Poland has needed some precise definition to answer the question "what do you mean by Poland?" It does not make things any easier that many place-names have also been changed from German to Polish.

For those parts of modern Poland which were included with Germany (or formerly Prussia) before 1918 (or 1945) the basic principles apply as for Germany. Genealogical societies in Germany relate to that area; the archives of a large part of the area (East Prussia) are in West Berlin. Silesian archives remain in modern Poland.

For those parts of modern Poland which were, before 1918, part of the Austro-Hungarian Empire (termed Galicia, although the boundaries were not precisely the same), this area was included politically with Hungary. Government vital records starting in 1895 should exist locally, but all church (including Jewish) registers up to 1895 are in Budapest, with microfilm of them in Salt Lake City. (This includes Ruthenia, awarded to

Czechoslovakia in 1918, claimed by Poland and Hungary, and now included in Russia.)

The remainder of Poland (commonly termed "Russian Poland" in the 19th century) was included in Tsarist Russia. This was the part of Poland from which the majority of Polish immigrants to America came, but it was no more than the majority. It is also this part of Poland to which the following refers, in general. The national archives comprise (records since 1918) *Archiwum Akt Nowych*, and (records before 1918) *Archiwum Glowne Akt Dawnych*; the address of both is Warsaw, Dluga 7, Poland. There are also 25 regional archives, whose holdings cover a vast range of subjects. The bulk of parish registers are of the Roman Catholic Church. They are kept in the parishes and no microfilming facility has been allowed to the LDS Genealogical Department. *LDS Research Paper C/31* is a guide to Polish research in English. See also "Polish-American Genealogical Research" (*Michigan Family Trails*, vol 4 no 1, Michigan Department of Education, 1972).

Portugal

Research in Portugal is not easy; recent political developments have not yet improved things. Government vital records are not centralized, but if you know the municipality or township, postal enquiries to the *Conservatoria de Registro Civil* in each town concerned will get results. Earlier records are in parish registers, which are virtually entirely Catholic, and retained in the parish churches. The national archives is *Arquivo Nacionalda Torre do Tombo*, Lisbon, Portugal. An extensive amount of earlier archives were lost in the great Lisbon earthquake of 1755.

Rumania

A large part of modern Rumania was formerly Transylvania, part of Hungary. The remainder was liberated from Turkish rule in the 1860s, comprising the two territories of Moldavia and Wallachia. Government vital records were introduced by making compulsory the keeping of parish registers by all churches – many were maintained voluntarily much earlier. Registrations are kept locally for 75 years in local offices and then transferred to the state archives : *Archivelor Statului*, B-Dul Gheorghe Gheorghui, Dej nr. 29, Bucharest. Like numerous other countries formerly under the Turkish Empire, there is a legacy of inadequate archives. The part of Rumania which was formerly Hungarian Transylvania is better recorded. Government vital records from 1895 are held locally, as elsewhere in former parts of Hungary, and all registers of all churches prior to 1895 are in Budapest, with microfilm of them in Salt Lake City.

Russia (USSR)

Most attempts at gaining access to genealogical material in Russia involve very wearying procedures, with no certainty of success. Even to obtain a civil registration certificate after the Revolution in date is likely to take up to a year; many attempts at getting earlier records than 1917 can be completely frustrated. The problem is the government attitude, not the records themselves.

The Russian Historical and Genealogical Society, 971 First Avenue, New York, NY 10022, has a large library of material. There are also other organizations working on the problem.

The best prospects are for the numerous foreign communities in Russia before the Revolution. For example, the British community there is well documented, and many of their records are in the LDS Genealogical Department computer file index. German communities in Russia are within the scope of *Arbeitsgemeinschaft ostdeutscher Familienforscher*, D 4330 Mulheim a.d.Ruhr-Saarn, Eibenkamp 23/25, Germany and of the *American Historical Society of Germans from Russia*, 615D

Street, Lincoln, Nebraska 68502.

It is worth remembering that some parts of what is now western Russia were under other government in the past. For example, those parts of the former Austro-Hungarian Empire which were officially part of Hungary and had their parish and other church registers called in to Budapest in 1895, are within the scope of records accessible outside Russia (*see* under HUNGARY).

Spain

Spanish archives are superb; Spain has had no political boundary charges of any significance for several centuries and there are no serious historical complications. For Americans (especially Latin Americans) the importance of Spain is as the mother country of South and Central America, except Brazil, and as the centre of the former Spanish empire. There are vast records of Latin America in Spanish archives. One should not forget that a wide sweep of land from Florida to California was at one time Spanish. Modern government vital records are not centralized, but held by each individual municipal court (*Juzado Municipal*), each of which handles postal enquiries. Parish registers are amongst the oldest in Europe; the earliest one starts in 1394. The General Office of Information of the Catholic Church in Spain produced a *Guidebook* in 1954. It lists all parishes in Spain, grouped in dioceses, with the date of the earliest surviving records they hold; in fact, an invaluable research tool. There are four national archives, each with a separate sphere of interest. *The National Historical Archives*, Madrid, are the modern central government archives. For ancestors who were resident in Spain – as distinct from the Spanish Empire – this should be the first of the four to visit. The next two mentioned are separate because Spain was, historically, a union of the two kingdoms of Castile and Aragon; hence we have the *Archives of Simancas* in Valladolid and the *Archives of the Crown of Aragon* in Barcelona. The most important for Latin American records are the Archives of the Indies (*Archivo de Indias*) in Seville. (The title "Indies" is a relic of Columbus's mistaken belief that he had discovered a new route to India, rather than a new continent – it is for the same reason, incidentally, that we talk of "Red Indians".) These are the archives of the Spanish Empire in the Americas. It includes, for example, early land records in Florida, Texas and California. It should be remembered that settlers from the United States were migrating while these places were still under Spanish control.

There is no detailed guide to Spanish genealogy published in English, but there is an organization which can help : *Instituto Internaciónal de Genealógia y Heráldica*, C/Atocha 94, Madrid, Spain.

Sweden

The Swedish Embassy (Watergate 600, 600 New Hampshire Avenue NW, Washington, DC 20037) issues free to enquirers a 28-page booklet *Tracing your Swedish Ancestry* which is very detailed and also nicely illustrated with photographs of original documents. Obtaining this should be the first step in any Swedish research program. There are also *LDS Research Papers D/3, D/14* and *D/15*.

Basically, parish registers are the primary source; as in Norway, the Established Church (Lutheran) has been delegated the task of keeping vital records (up to 1946). With very few exceptions, all of these are in the district or municipal archives. There are 17 of these and, in addition, there are seven other archives of a more national than regional nature. In addition to the births or baptisms, marriages and deaths or burials which can be found recorded in parish registers everywhere, the Swedish parish records have one special feature. This is that Swedish ministers made regular visits to and kept records of everyone in the parish, of arrivals and departures, their health and behaviour, in fascinating detail. As in Norway, the police at the major ports kept details of emigrants; these have been indexed recently. Although Swedish vital records are spread in district archives, it is worth knowing that all vital records after 1860, together with all lists of emigrants and their origins and destinations, are also available in a consolidated series in the central bureau of statistics, *Statistiska centralbyrån*, Fack, Karlavägen 100, S-102 50 Stockholm. Any researches which involve an emigrant from Sweden after 1860 would probably be best if they were started at this office.

Switzerland

Politically Switzerland is a federation of cantons, each of which is to some extent separate, and this is reflected in the records. There are also strong family ties which maintain a strong interest in genealogy. Some cantons had started as early as 1820 to keep government vital records, but a uniform policy began in 1848 of delegating this to the churches, who were required to keep the records by law. In 1876, this was changed to a civil process. The civil registrar of each town will prepare a family record (*Familienschein*) from his registers. Earlier records are in parish registers, most of which start around the year 1600. There is a splendid guide to locating surnames in Switzerland, the *Familiennamenbuch der Schweiz*, which locates all Swiss surnames by canton and by date.

Almost all Swiss parish registers before 1800, with other records, are in cantonal archives. The *Swiss National Archives* are at Archivstrasse 4, 3003 Bern, Switzerland; there are also the *Episcopal Archives* in Basel, with many of the church records – not so much registers as administrative records.

A guide on Swiss records in English is *LDS Research Paper D/2*.

Yugoslavia

Historically, Yugoslavia is a modern creation, bringing together territories with very different pasts, different religions and different records. Parts in the north and east – notably the Voivodina and Slovenia – were part of Hungary in 1895. Therefore all church registers before 1895 are in Budapest and on microfilm in Salt Lake City. This area is largely Roman Catholic in denomination and used the Roman alphabet generally employed in America and western Europe.

Further east, the country spent a long period under Turkish rule. The Christian population is largely Eastern Orthodox rather than Catholic, and uses the Cyrillic alphabet. The situation is further complicated as quite a proportion of the population is Muslim, which makes for an entirely distinct factor in research.

There were no government vital records kept before 1946, other than in the area referred to above. Earlier records, such as exist, are supposed to be collected into regional archives. It is usually recommended that employing an attorney is the best way to accomplish research in Yugoslavia. Unless one is employed who speaks the appropriate language (which varies) and also English, problems may ensue. The professional body, which can supply names and addresses of attorneys, is *Udruzenje Pravnika FNRJ*, Beograd, Proleterskih Brigada 74, Yugoslavia. There is also the Organization of the Serbian Emigrants; *Matica iseljenika Srbije*, Nusiceva 4, 11000 Beograd, Yugoslavia. (The exact function of this organization is not clear, but they have government support.)